# Cambridge Elements

Elements in Applied Social Psychology
edited by
**Susan Clayton**
*College of Wooster, Ohio*

# THE PSYCHOLOGY OF CLIMATE CHANGE ADAPTATION

Anne van Valkengoed
*University of Groningen*
Linda Steg
*University of Groningen*

**CAMBRIDGE**
**UNIVERSITY PRESS**

University Printing House, Cambridge CB2 8BS, United Kingdom

One Liberty Plaza, 20th Floor, New York, NY 10006, USA

477 Williamstown Road, Port Melbourne, VIC 3207, Australia

314–321, 3rd Floor, Plot 3, Splendor Forum, Jasola District Centre, New Delhi – 110025, India

79 Anson Road, #06–04/06, Singapore 079906

Cambridge University Press is part of the University of Cambridge.

It furthers the University's mission by disseminating knowledge in the pursuit of education, learning, and research at the highest international levels of excellence.

www.cambridge.org
Information on this title: www.cambridge.org/9781108724456
DOI: 10.1017/9781108595438



First published 2019

*A catalogue record for this publication is available from the British Library.*

ISBN 978-1-108-72445-6 Paperback
ISSN 2631-777X (Online)
ISSN 2631-7761 (Print)

# The Psychology of Climate Change Adaptation

Elements in Applied Social Psychology

DOI: 10.1017/9781108595438
First published online: May 2019

---

Anne van Valkengoed
*University of Groningen*

Linda Steg
*University of Groningen*

**Author for correspondence:** Anne van Valkengoed, a.m.van.valkengoed@rug.nl

**Abstract:** Why do some people adapt to the risks of climate change, while others do not? This Element provides an in-depth overview of the psychology of climate change adaptation. It begins with an overview of adaptation behaviour and highlights the importance of successful adaptation by individuals and households. Key psychological theories are introduced that can explain adaptation behaviour and the role of a wide variety of motivational variables in adaptation behaviour is discussed, such as risk perception, experiences with climate-related hazards, and perceived responsibility. Next, the authors examine three examples of how this psychological knowledge has been used to develop and test interventions to promote adaptation behaviour in real-world settings. After this, the relationship between climate adaptation behaviour and climate mitigation behaviour is considered, and the potential for integrating these bodies of literature is put forward. This Element concludes with an agenda for future psychological research on climate change adaptation behaviour.

**Keywords:** climate change adaptation, risk perception, disaster risk reduction, protection motivation theory, households, climate change



ISBNs: 9781108724456 (PB), 9781108595438 (OC)
ISSNs: 2631-777X (online), ISSN 2631-7761 (print)

# Contents

# 1 Introduction

Climate change is already affecting our lives. Global temperature has on average increased by 1°C since the beginning of the Industrial Revolution (IPCC, 2018). Moreover, it has now become unavoidable that the climate will change even further (IPCC, 2014c). Even if we completely halted all greenhouse gas emissions right now, sea levels and global temperature levels would continue to rise for the next decades (Solomon, Plattner, Knutti, & Friedlingstein, 2008). Climate change will increase the frequency and severity of a wide variety of natural hazards, including heatwaves, flooding, drought, tropical cyclones, hurricanes, vector-borne diseases, landslides, hailstorms, and wildfires. Such climate-related hazards threaten human health and well-being and can cause severe economic damage (Sauerborn & Ebi, 2012).

Because climate change is unavoidable, it is no longer sufficient to only focus our efforts on limiting or reducing it. It is also critical that people take actions to protect themselves against the impacts of climate-related hazards. Examples of actions that people can undertake include, amongst others, clearing the fire-prone foliage around their house to reduce the risk of wildfire, purchasing flood insurance, painting their home in a lighter colour to reflect sunlight and lower indoor temperatures during a heatwave, preparing an emergency kit, and actively following weather forecasts so that timely actions can be taken. Additionally, people can support adaptive policies that are aimed at defending them and others against climate-related hazards. Such actions are referred to as "adaptation to climate change" (IPCC, 2014b).

Despite the urgency and effectiveness of adaptation actions in reducing or avoiding the negative impacts of climate-related hazards, many people still fail to take the necessary measures to protect themselves (Basolo et al., 2008). Estimates are that approximately half the households that are at significant risk of flooding in the United Kingdom have undertaken no actions to prepare themselves against flood risks (Bichard & Kazmierczak, 2012), while another study found that 82.1 per cent of participants in the United Kingdom were not prepared for flooding (Soane et al., 2010). Promoting adaptation behaviour amongst individuals and households is one of the critical challenges of the twenty-first century.

In this Element, we provide a social psychological perspective on climate change adaptation behaviour. We discuss literature that applies theory and insights from social psychology to understand which factors explain whether individuals and households are likely to protect themselves against the risks of climate change. By building on fundamental principles and theories of individual and group behaviour, social psychology is uniquely equipped to explain and predict how individuals and groups adapt to climate change. Additionally, social psychological research plays a key role in evaluating and explaining which interventions are effective in changing people's behaviour, such as engaging in climate change adaptation. As we will show in this Element, the social psychological perspective on climate change adaptation provides critical insights into understanding and changing how individuals adapt to climate change.

This Element is organised as follows. In Section 2, we start with discussing what is meant by climate change adaptation and which individual and household behaviours may be considered adaptive. In Section 3, we review the literature on which psychological variables are related to adaptation behaviour. We introduce the Model of Private Proactive Adaptation to Climate Change and an extension of this model, and we review empirical evidence on the extent to which the variables included in these models predict adaptive behaviour. In Section 4, we review interventions that demonstrate how adaptation can be promoted by applying psychological theory. In Section 5, we discuss the commonalities and differences between climate change adaptation and climate change mitigation, which focus on adapting to versus preventing climate change, respectively. In Section 6, we propose a research agenda that highlights key gaps in the literature and identifies directions for future research, including possible theoretical advancements and methodological improvements.

## 2 What Is Climate Change Adaptation?

*Climate change adaptation* is defined as 'the process of adjustment to actual or expected climate and its effects. In human systems, adaptation seeks to moderate or avoid harm or exploit beneficial opportunities' (IPCC, 2014b). In this section, we focus on adaptation to natural hazards that are likely to increase in severity and frequency due to climate change, such as heatwaves, flooding, and droughts. As such, we define *adaptation* as 'behaviours that are aimed at avoiding or reducing the negative impacts of climate change'. It has often been argued that climate change mitigation, the process of halting or minimizing climate change, should take precedence over climate change adaptation (Pielke, Prins, Rayner, & Sarewitz, 2007). However, as previous mitigation actions have proven to be insufficient, the impacts of climate change are now unavoidable. Today, adaptation to climate change is recognised as an important component of the response to climate change, complementary to climate change mitigation (IPCC, 2014d).

Different types of adaptation can be distinguished. First, a distinction can be made between reactive adaptation and anticipatory adaptation. *Anticipatory adaptation* refers to adaptive actions taken in response to expected climate-related hazards, while *reactive adaptation* occurs in response to climate-related hazards that have already occurred (Smit, Burton, Klein, & Wandel, 2000). Second, *autonomous adaptation* refers to adaptive actions undertaken by private actors without the interference of governments or other public bodies. *Planned adaptation* on the other hand refers to policy decisions made by public bodies (Tol, Klein, & Nicholls, 2008). Third, *incremental adaptation* refers to adaptive actions that aim to maintain the status quo and the current way of life, while *transformational adaptation* subsumes adaptive actions that fundamentally alter existing institutional, governance, and value systems (IPCC, 2014a). Fourth, a distinction can be made between adaptation and *maladaptation*. The latter refers to 'actions, or inaction that may lead to increased risk of adverse climate-related outcomes, increased vulnerability to climate change, or diminished welfare, now or in the future' (IPCC, 2014a, p. 857). Examples of maladaptation include denying or minimizing the problem, wishful thinking, fatalism (Grothmann & Patt, 2005), or actions that may offer protection from climate change in the short term but increase vulnerability in the long term (Barnett & O'Neill, 2010). For example, island inhabitants in the Philippines use coral stone to raise their floors and reduce the impacts from flooding (Jamero et al., 2017). However, coral plays an important role in regulating water levels; removing it increases vulnerability to flooding in the long term (Ferrario et al., 2014). Maladaptation also includes actions that increase greenhouse gas emissions (Barnett & O'Neill, 2010). Examples include desalinisation of water to adapt to drought or using air-conditioning to cope with heatwaves (Barnett & O'Neill, 2010). These examples indicate that adaptation and mitigation are related, and that possible synergies and trade-offs between adaptation and mitigation may occur (R. J. T. Klein et al., 2007). We will return to this topic later in this Element.

## 2.1 Adaptation by Individuals and Households

The process of adaptation to climate change needs to take place at all levels of society and can be initiated by local, national, and international governments, as well as by industry, communities, households, and individuals (Adger, 2001; Adger, Arnell, & Tompkins, 2005). While the literature on adaptation to climate change has mostly focused on planned adaptation, that is, adaptation measures implemented by governments, we focus on adaptation to climate change by households and individuals. Following the previously discussed definitions, we thus focus on adaptation behaviours that are autonomous, mostly incremental, and that may be either reactive or anticipatory. Household actions are more likely to be incremental, as transformational adaptation requires large-scale societal changes that may be more difficult to establish by individuals and households alone. Additionally, we focus on adaptive behaviour, as hardly any studies have been conducted on maladaptive behaviour at the level of individuals and households; we return to this topic when we discuss the research agenda.

It is critical to focus on adaptation behaviour of individuals and households, and not to rely only on large-scale, government-issued protective measures, as governments alone cannot guarantee successful adaptation (Takao et al., 2004). Government-issued adaptive measures will typically leave a margin of error referred to as 'residual risk' (Aliagha, Jin, Choong, Nadzri Jaafar, & Ali, 2014). For example, the Netherlands is a flood-prone country where many people live below sea level and are protected by dykes. Currently, not all dykes have the same safety level, which is expressed as the probability of a flood occurring in a particular year in that area. The highest safety level is 1/10,000 years, while the lowest safety level is 1/1,250 years (Aerts, 2009). Raising all the dykes to provide the highest safety level for flooding would be extremely costly. Cost-benefit analyses show that the most cost-effective safety level for most dykes in the Netherlands is indeed much lower than the highest possible level (Kind, 2014). As this example shows, government policy to manage climate risks never accounts fully for all risk, as it would be extremely costly to do so. Especially since climate-related hazards will occur more frequently in the future, individual adaptation actions are of critical importance.

As indicated earlier, governments base their risk management strategies on cost-benefit analyses (Baan & Klijn, 2004). Such analyses also show that individual actions to adapt to climate change can be highly effective in reducing the impacts of climate-related hazards while incurring relatively low costs (Bates, Quick, & Kloss, 2009; Botzen, Aerts, & van den Bergh, 2009). For example, one study found that flood-adapted building use (i.e. not placing expensive furniture and equipment in the lower stories and cellar of a building) and flood-adapted interior fitting (i.e. using waterproof building materials and easily movable furniture) reduced flood damage ratios by 46 per cent and 53 per cent, respectively (Kreibich et al., 2005). Another study estimated that monetary damage from floods could be reduced by up to 80 per cent through individual adaptation actions, such as moving furniture or temporarily sealing openings in the house with sandbags (Egli, 2002, cited in Grothmann & Reusswig, 2006). Governments therefore increasingly acknowledge that behaviour by individuals and households forms an essential component of climate adaptation strategies (Baan & Klijn, 2004; Elrick-Barr, Smith, Preston, Thomsen, & Baum, 2016). For example, the United Kingdom's

National Adaptation Programme states, 'if adapting to climate change is in the private interests of an individual . . . then it should occur naturally and without the government's intervention' (DEFRA, 2013, p. 7, quoted in Porter, Dessai, & Tompkins, 2014).

Having identified the importance of adaptation at the individual and household levels, the next critical question is what adaptation actions can be taken by individuals and households. It is almost impossible to present an exhaustive list of adaptive behaviours that households and individuals could perform. Indeed, one study presented more than 100 adaptive actions that households in Sweden could conduct (Wamsler & Brink, 2014). Importantly, different geographical areas are faced with different climate-related risks and therefore require unique adaptive responses. Rather than presenting an exhaustive list, we therefore use a categorisation to identify the most commonly studied adaptive actions at the level of individuals and households. Our categorisation is composed of six categories of adaptive behaviours that may be conducted by individuals and households to protect themselves against climate-related hazards: information seeking, preparative actions, protective actions, evacuating, purchasing insurance, and political actions. Please note that this categorisation was informed by the literature review we conducted for this Element and was therefore not developed a priori on theoretical grounds. As such, this categorisation may not be complete; we come back to this when we discuss the research agenda. An overview of the categorisation used for this Element is provided in Table 1.

**Table 1** Classification of different types of adaptive behaviours that individuals and households can undertake

| Type of adaptive behaviour | Description | Examples |
|---|---|---|
| Information seeking | Expending time and effort to gain more information about specific climate-related hazards, to identify whether you are at risk of a hazard, and gaining information on which actions to perform to successfully adapt to climate change | Studying weather forecasts, using flood maps, looking up information on how to flood-proof the house, reading government brochures on preparedness, listening to the radio during a climate-related hazard |

**Table 1** (cont.)

| Type of adaptive behaviour | Description | Examples |
|---|---|---|
| Preparative actions | Structural actions taken before the onset of a climate-related hazard aimed at reducing the probability of being affected by a hazard or minimising its negative impact | Boarding up windows before a hurricane, installing valves with back-flow prevention, cleaning gutters, storing non-perishable foods |
| Protective actions | Actions taken during an ongoing climate-related hazard to avoid or reduce its impact | Defending the home against wildfire, not driving through floodwater with a vehicle, staying inside during a hurricane, staying cool during a heatwave |
| Evacuation | Temporarily moving away from an area to avoid the negative impacts of climate-related hazard; may also include leaving an area permanently if required | Complying with government-issued evacuation, planned retreat, migration |
| Purchasing insurance | Purchasing an insurance policy that covers losses from one or multiple climate-related hazards | Flood insurance, wildfire insurance, homeowner insurance |
| Political actions | Influencing local or national governments to implement adaptation policies | Voting in favour of adaptive policies, protesting, participating in town hall meetings, forming an action group, signing a petition |

*Information seeking.* An important part of reducing the impacts of climate-related hazards is to be aware of whether you are at risk. Information seeking can be defined as 'a deliberate effort to acquire information in response to a need or gap in one's knowledge' (Kievik & Gutteling, 2011, p. 1477). Information seeking is often conceptualised as an initial phase or first step in the process of hazard adjustment (P. D. Howe, 2011). People may start seeking information before or after a climate-related hazard has occurred (Griffin et al., 2008). People can also look up information on immediate weather forecasts or government-issued weather warnings. This information can help people determine whether a natural hazard is imminent, and whether and which urgent responses are required. Governments frequently provide information about the risk of hazards such as flooding and wildfires that a residential area faces. The Federal Emergency Management Agency (FEMA) in the United States issues flood maps that showcase long-term flood probabilities for residential areas (Xian, Lin, & Hatzikyriakou, 2015). Many governments also provide checklists, information sheets, or websites that indicate what actions are appropriate to adapt to specific climate-related hazards. Such information may help people prepare effectively.

*Preparative actions.* Preparative actions are structural actions taken before the onset of a climate-related hazard and are aimed at reducing the probability of being affected by a hazard or minimizing its negative impacts. Examples of preparative actions include installing hurricane shutters, trimming fire-prone foliage around the house, preparing an emergency kit, applying heat-reflecting paint to the home, and purchasing sandbags to avoid floodwater entering the home. These measures are usually more cost and time intensive than the other behaviours described here and require deliberate preparation.

*Protective actions.* Protective actions include all behaviours that are conducted during a climate-related hazard to avoid or reduce its negative impacts. This may include avoiding physical labour during a heatwave, moving to a cellar during a hurricane, reducing water consumption during a drought, or moving upstairs during a flood. These actions are taken in response to ongoing hazards and are therefore usually more intuitive and less planned for than preparative actions, even though some protective actions can also be planned beforehand.

*Evacuation.* For some climate-related hazards, negative consequences may be best avoided by temporarily evacuating. For example, governments recommend evacuation in response to strong hurricanes or wildfires. Migration, that is, permanent relocation, may also be an adaptive action if conditions become too extreme due to climate change (McLeman & Smit, 2006). Some island communities may be forced to relocate to the mainland in the future because of rising sea levels and inundation (Burkett, 2011). Migration has been suggested as an effective way to improve resilience in such circumstances (Black, Bennett, Thomas, & Beddington, 2011). Yet, migration is often associated with significant losses of community, sense of place, and cultural heritage. For example, many Native American communities, particularly in coastal areas such as in Alaska and Louisiana, may have to migrate from areas that hold important cultural and historical significance (Maldonado, Shearer, Bronen, Peterson, & Lazrus, 2013). Migration may not solve all issues caused by climate change. A study in Cambodia found that migration for climate reasons did not always achieve the goal of reducing food insecurity, which could lead to a vicious cycle of food insecurity and migration that reinforces poverty over the long term (Jacobson, Crevello, Chea, & Jarihani, 2019). It is therefore disputed to what extent migration represents successful adaptation to climate change (de Sherbinin et al., 2011).

*Purchasing insurance.* Purchasing insurance may be an effective way to reduce the financial costs associated with coping with the negative impacts of climate-related hazards. This adaptive action however has its limits, as it only protects against financial costs and does not offer protection against personal physical damage, injury, or the emotional damage associated with experiencing a natural hazard (Siegrist & Gutscher, 2008). Yet, insurance may be critical for low-income households that are faced with repeating natural hazards that may contribute to the perpetuation of the cycle of poverty (Mechler, Linnerooth-Bayer, & Peppiatt, 2006).

*Political actions.* As mentioned previously, adaptive actions can also be initiated by local, national, and international governments. In democratic countries, individuals and households can be actively engaged in the development and implementation of adaptation policy. For example, people may vote in favour of or against government-level adaptive policies or parties that support them (Hagen, Middel, & Pijawka, 2016). People may also attempt to convince their government representatives to implement more adaptive measures (Elrick-Barr et al., 2016). Furthermore, people can influence government policies through forms of protest or collective action, although, to the best of our knowledge, these actions have not been studied in the context of climate change adaptation.

In the next section, we discuss studies that examine how different psychological variables relate to whether people engage in these types of actions. To preserve the readability of the Element, we do not discuss the results for each type of adaptive behaviour separately. Rather, we talk about adaptation or adaptive behaviour in general, which we use as an umbrella term to refer to the previously mentioned behaviours. However, it is important to keep in mind that some psychological predictors may be more or less important than others for some adaptive behaviours. We return to this topic in the research agenda.

## 3 Factors That Promote Adaptation Behaviour

In this section, we review the psychological literature on adaptation. We introduce fifteen psychological variables that could be related to climate change adaptation. We discuss the theoretical rationale explaining why variables may be related to adaptation behaviour and review the associated empirical evidence.[1] We first introduce the Model of Private Proactive Adaptation to Climate Change (MPPACC; Grothmann & Patt, 2005, see Figure 1). Based on protection motivation theory, the MPPACC proposes that four key components predict adaptation behaviour: risk perception, self-efficacy, outcome efficacy, and perceived costs of adapting. The MPPACC also includes three additional variables, namely experience with climate-related hazards, trust in government measures, and perceived incentives to adapt. Next, we introduce an extension of the MPPACC model proposed by Dang, Li, and Bruwer (2012) (see Figure 1) that contains four additional variables: social norms, negative affect, climate change perceptions, and habits. Last, we introduce four variables that were not included in these theoretical models but that have been examined in the adaptation literature frequently. These variables are place attachment, knowledge, personal responsibility for adaptation, and trust in the government. Table 2 provides an overview of the variables that we discuss, the main conclusions from the literature review, and key references .

In this review, we discuss in depth the different studies for each psychological variable. For a meta-analytic overview of the relative importance of the discussed variables in climate change adaptation, please see Van Valkengoed & Steg (2019).

### 3.1 The Model of Private Proactive Adaptation to Climate Change

The MPPACC has been developed to explain which factors motivate individuals and households to engage in adaptation behaviour (Grothmann & Patt, 2005). The model is an extension of protection motivation theory (Rogers, 1975, 1983), which has been used extensively in the domain of health psychology to explain how people cope with health-related threats, such as smoking (Yan et al., 2014), engaging in physical exercise

[1] We would like to highlight that many of the studies we discuss were conducted in a Western context, and results may therefore not be generalizable to all contexts. We discuss this in more detail in the discussion section.

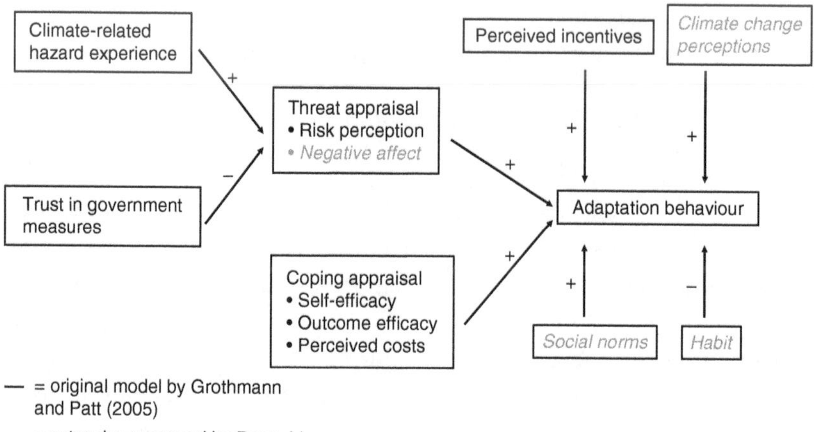


**Figure 1** The model of private proactive adaptation to climate change (adapted from Grothmann & Patt, 2005) and the extension proposed by Dang, Li, and Bruwer (2012) in italic.

**Source:** Figure made by authors.

(Bui, Mullan, & McCaffery, 2013), and choosing to undergo cancer screenings (Bai et al., 2018). As climate change adaptation also involves coping with threats, the protection motivation framework seems relevant to explain which factors motivate adaptive behaviour. The MPPACC was developed to adapt the protection motivation framework employed in health psychology to explain climate change adaptation. Similar to protection motivation theory, the MPPACC proposes that four factors predict people's adaptation behaviour: risk perception (referred to as the 'threat appraisal') and self-efficacy, outcome efficacy, and perceived adaptation costs (jointly referred to as the 'coping appraisal'). We discuss each component in turn before looking at the interrelationship between these variables as assumed in these models.

### *3.1.1 Risk Perception*

*Risk perception* is defined as people's subjective judgements of the likelihood and consequences of a hazard harming them or someone/something they value, such as family members, close others, possessions, or nature (Paek & Hove, 2017). Perceiving high risks results in an uncomfortable state of mind that people want to reduce. Risk perception is therefore likely to motivate people to undertake adaptive actions. This is also referred to as the 'motivational hypothesis' (Weinstein, Rothman, & Nicolich, 1998). The greater the

**Table 2** A summary of the literature review per variable

| Variable | Definition | Summary of literature review | Key reference |
|---|---|---|---|
| Risk perception | People's subjective judgements of the likelihood and consequences of a hazard harming them or someone/something they value | Risk perception has been extensively studied in the literature. Despite this, the findings are still strongly mixed, with many studies reporting positive or nonsignificant effects. Aspects that may influence the relationship with adaptation are study design, measurement of risk perception, and interaction with other variables. | Wachinger, Renn, Begg, & Kuhlicke (2013). The risk perception paradox – implications for governance and communication of natural hazards. *Risk Anal., 33*(6), 1049–1065. |
| Self-efficacy | A person's perception of their own ability to engage in adaptive behaviour | Overall, self-efficacy is positively associated with adaptive behaviour. There are some studies that find a nonsignificant effect. This may be attributed to the fact that some behaviours are perceived as so easy to perform that all participants perceive their self-efficacy as high. | Burnham & Ma (2017). Climate change adaptation: Factors influencing Chinese smallholder farmers' perceived self-efficacy and adaptation intent. *Reg. Environ. Change, 17,* 171–186. |
| Outcome efficacy | People's perceptions of the effectiveness or utility of a measure or behaviour in protecting them from a climate-related hazard | Most studies find that outcome efficacy predicts adaptation behaviour. There are also studies that do not find a significant relationship, but it is not immediately clear why this occurs. Outcome efficacy can also influence which type of adaptive action people undertake. | Samaddar, Chatterjee, Misra, & Tatano (2014). Outcome-expectancy and self-efficacy: Reasons or results of flood preparedness intention? *Int. J. Disaster Risk Reduct. 8,* 91–99. |

**Table 2** (cont.)

| Variable | Definition | Summary of literature review | Key reference |
|---|---|---|---|
| Perceived costs | The costs that people perceive to be involved with taking adaptive actions | The results for perceived costs are mixed. Whereas some studies report a positive correlation, other studies find a null effect. One study suggests that perceived costs are likely more important for more expensive adaptive measures, rather than low-cost measures. | Terpstra & Lindell (2012). Citizens' perceptions of flood hazard adjustment: An application of the Protective Action Decision Model. *Environ Behav, 45*(8), 993–1018. |
| Experience with climate-related hazards | The extent to which people have experienced climate-related hazards | The results for experience with climate-related hazards are mixed, with positive, non-significant, and negative results reported in the literature. The measurement of the experience as either a yes-or-no measure or the intensity of the experience does not seem to account for the heterogeneous findings. The near-miss experience may play an important role in explaining some of these contradictory findings. | Demski, Capstick, Pidgeon, Sposato, & Spence (2017). Experience of extreme weather affects climate change mitigation and adaptation responses. *Clim. Chang., 140,* 149–164. |
| Trust in government-issued adaptive measures | The extent to which people trust that government-implemented adaptive measures will protect them from climate-related measures | Most studies find a non-significant relationship between trust in government-issued measures and adaptation behaviour. The 'levee-effect', which assumes that trust in government measures should be negatively associated with adaptive behaviour, is therefore not supported. When government measures are informative rather than structural, trust in measures can also be positively associated with adaptation. | Terpstra (2011). Emotions, trust, and perceived risk: Affective and cognitive routes to flood preparedness behavior. *Risk Anal. 31*(10), 1658–1675. |

| | | | |
|---|---|---|---|
| Perceived incentives | The extent to which people perceive incentives to adapt, other than reducing the impacts of climate change | Only one study has examined this variable, which found that perceived incentives were positively associated with adaptive behaviour. | Dang, Li, Nuberg & Brewer (2014). Understanding farmers' adaptation intention to climate change: A structural equation modelling study in the Mekong Delta, Vietnam. *Environ. Sci. Policy, 41,* 11–22. |
| Social norms | Perceptions of what other people perceive as appropriate conduct (injunctive norms) and perceptions of what others are doing (descriptive norms) | Almost all studies support that descriptive and injunctive norms are associated with adaptation. For injunctive norms, the direction of the norms matters (i.e. whether other people approve or disapprove of adaptive behaviour). Descriptive norms can inform people's perceptions of self- and outcome efficacy of adaptive behaviour. | Lo (2013). The role of social norms in climate adaptation: Mediating risk perception and flood insurance purchase. *Glob. Environ. Chang., 23,* 1249–1257. |
| Negative emotions | Negative feelings that people can experience in response to climate change or climate-related hazards, such as fear, concern, and worry | Most studies find that concern about climate change or climate-related hazards is positively associated with engaging in adaptation. The results for fear and worry are mixed, with studies reporting positive or non-significant findings. The assumption that strong negative affect can undermine adaptive behaviour was not supported. Positive affect however may inhibit adaptation. | Terpstra (2011). Emotions, trust, and perceived risk: Affective and cognitive routes to flood preparedness behaviour. *Risk Anal. 31*(10), 1658–1675. |

**Table 2** (cont.)

| Variable | Definition | Summary of literature review | Key reference |
|---|---|---|---|
| Climate change perceptions | The way people understand climate change and what people perceive to be its essential components. Usually assessed as perceptions of the reality, causes, and consequences of climate change | Most studies find that belief in the reality of climate change is usually not associated with adaptation. Higher levels of scepticism regarding climate change have been found to be associated with lowered levels of adaptation behaviour and policy support. Especially the perceived negative consequences of climate change have been found to be positively associated with adaptation behaviour. Results are different for farmers, who are generally more skeptical of climate change but still adapt to its consequences. | Brenkert-Smith, Meldrum, & Champ (2015). Climate change beliefs and hazard mitigation behaviors: Homeowners and wildfire risk. *Environ. Hazard. 14*(4), 341–360. |
| Habits | Behaviours that people perform without thinking if they find themselves in specific situations | Only one study has examined this relationship and found that habits did not form a barrier to adaptation: farmers who reported that their farming behaviour was more habitual were more likely to have the intention to engage in adaptive farming. | Dang, Li, Nuberg, & Brewer (2014). Understanding farmers' adaptation intention to climate change: A structural equation modelling study in the Mekong Delta, Vietnam. *Environ. Sci. Policy, 41,* 11–22. |
| Place attachment | The emotional connection that people have to a place | Most studies find a positive relationship between place attachment and adaptation behaviour. Yet, place attachment can also form a barrier when people do not want to evacuate, when the required adaptive actions | Bonaiuto, Alves, de Dominicis, & Petruccelli (2016). Place attachment and natural hazard risk: Research review and agenda. *J. Environ. Psychol. 48*, 33–53. |

| | | | |
|---|---|---|---|
| | | harm the meaning of a place, and by lowering perceptions of risk. | |
| Trust in governments | People's general trust in government and the government's ability to cope with climate-related hazards | Most studies find a positive correlation between trust and adaptive behaviour, but studies have also reported negative and nonsignificant findings. | Absher & Vaske (2011). The role of trust in residents' fire wise actions. *Int. J. Wildland Fire, 20*, 318–325. |
| Knowledge | People's factual understanding (objective knowledge) about climate change or climate-related hazards, or self-assessed knowledge (subjective knowledge) | Studies report mixed findings regarding the relationship between objective knowledge and adaptation, with studies reporting positive, negative, and non-significant findings. Objective knowledge may inhibit specific adaptive behaviours, such as information seeking. Subjective knowledge is generally positively associated with adaptation behaviour. | Bates, Quick, & Kloss (2009). Antecedents of intention to help mitigate wildfire: Implications for campaigns promoting wildfire mitigation to the general public in the wildland-urban interface. *Saf. Sci., 47,* 374–381. |
| Responsibility | Perceived personal responsibility to adapt to climate change | For personal adaptation behaviours, perceived personal responsibility is mostly positively associated with adaptation behaviour, while perceived government responsibility is negatively associated. For policy support, both perceived personal responsibility and perceived government responsibility are positively associated with support. | Terpstra & Gutteling (2008). Household perceived responsibilities in flood risk management in the Netherlands. *Int. J. Water. Resour. D., 24*(4), 555–565. |

discrepancy between a desired outcome state and the perceived risk, the more 'motivational energy' people would have to address the perceived risk (Grothmann & Patt, 2005).

The relationship between risk perception and adaptation has been examined since the 1970s, and a large number of papers on this topic have been published. While a positive relationship between risk perception and adaptation behaviour as predicted by the motivational hypothesis appears intuitive, the empirical evidence on this relationship is not consistent. Whereas many papers indeed find that higher levels of risk perceptions are associated with more adaptive behaviour (Botzen, Aerts, & van den Bergh, 2013; Dang, Li, Nuberg, & Bruwer, 2014; Elrick-Barr et al., 2016; Esham & Garforth, 2013; Feng, Liu, Huo, & Ma, 2017; Grothmann & Reusswig, 2006; Kalkstein & Sheridan, 2007; Koerth, Jones, et al., 2013; Liu et al., 2013; Singh, Zwickle, Bruskotter, & Wilson, 2017), there are also many papers that find no significant relationship (e.g. Collins, 2008; Horney, MacDonald, Van Willigen, Berke, & Kaufman, 2010; Lazo, Waldman, Morrow, & Thacher, 2010; Lo, Xu, Chan, & Su, 2015; McGee, 2005; Morss et al., 2016; Price, McFarlane, & Lantz, 2016; Rauf et al., 2017; Semenza, Ploubidis, & George, 2011) or that even find a negative relationships between risk perception and adaptive behaviour, where those who perceived more risk were less likely to undertake adaptive measures (Burnham & Ma, 2017; Ejeta, Ardalan, Paton, & Yaseri, 2016; H.-C. Hung, 2009; Thaker, Maibach, Leiserowitz, Zhao, & Howe, 2016). The relationship between risk perception and adaptive behaviour is thus debated, and a consensus has not yet been achieved in the literature (Wachinger, Renn, Begg, & Kuhlicke, 2013).

Some explanations for the divergent findings have been offered. First, the contradictory findings may be attributable to the methodology used in some correlational studies. The motivational hypothesis states that the perception of risks motivates behavioural change, which implies that risk perception is assumed to precede adaptive behaviour (Basolo et al., 2008; Weinstein et al., 1998). Yet, some correlational studies measure *current* levels of risk perception and *past* adaptive behaviours, meaning that there is a mismatch in the temporal order of the variables that can explain the non-significant effects that have been observed in the literature (Weinstein et al., 1998). Furthermore, as performing an adaptive behaviour can actually lower levels of risk perception, correlating current levels of risk perception with past adaptive behaviour may also explain the negative relationships reported in the literature (Weinstein et al., 1998). A solution to address this issue is to correlate current levels of risk perception with intended, rather than already performed, adaptive behaviours, or to use longitudinal designs to correlate current levels of risk perception at Time 1 with adaptive behaviours at Time 2 (Bubeck & Botzen, 2013). Indeed, some studies suggest that risk perception is more predictive of future or intended behaviours rather than past behaviours (Bubeck, Botzen, & Aerts, 2012). For example, risk perception predicted planned, but not already implemented, flood risk reduction measures in a French study (Richert, Erdlenbruch, & Figuières, 2017). Yet, this effect has not been observed in all studies (e.g. Poussin, Botzen, & Aerts, 2014). Therefore, this explanation cannot account for all observed heterogeneity between studies.

Another explanation for the divergent findings in the literature pertains to the measurement of risk perception. Different operationalisations of risk perception have been employed in the literature, which may account for some of the heterogeneity in results across studies (Basolo et al., 2008). For example, many studies employ the classic 'probability x consequence' operationalisation of risk perception and assess the perceived probability of a hazard occurring and the perceived consequences of that hazard (Breakwell, 2010). Some studies have found that it is specifically the perception of consequences, and not probability, that predicts adaptive behaviour (Lo & Chan, 2017; McNeill, Dunlop, Heath, Skinner, & Morrison, 2013; van Duinen, Filatova, Geurts, & van der Veen, 2015). Yet, some studies have also found the opposite result, namely that perceived probability was more predictive of adaptive behaviour than perceived consequences (Bubeck, Botzen, Suu, & Aerts, 2012; Terpstra, 2011). The spatial distance of the risks studied may also matter. Specifically, proximal risk perceptions (i.e. perceiving that a hazard will occur close by) best predicted personal intentions to adapt, whereas distal risk perceptions (i.e. perceiving that a hazard will occur far away) best predicted support for adaptation policies (Brügger, Morton, & Dessai, 2015). Lastly, it may be important to specifically think about the element or aspect of a hazard to which the risk perception measure pertains. One study found that perceived risk of flooding, rather than perceived risk of winds, motivated people to evacuate from a hurricane (Whitehead et al., 2000). The conceptualisation of the risk perception measure may therefore play a role in whether a significant relationship is found between risk perception and adaptation.

The relationship between risk perception and adaptation behaviour could also depend on moderating variables. A literature review suggests three reasons why risk perception may not translate into adaptive behaviour (Wachinger et al., 2013). First, some individuals may simply accept the risk and consider that the benefits of engaging in adaptive behaviour do not outweigh the costs. Second, some individuals may perceive risks but believe that it is not their responsibility to prevent the impacts of climate-related hazards. Third, some people may not have the resources to act in the appropriate manner in response to the perceived risk or may lack the knowledge of which actions are appropriate. We discuss the influence of perceived adaptation costs, trust, responsibility, and knowledge of adaptive behaviour later in this review.

A final reason why risk perception may sometimes not translate into adaptation behaviour goes back to the original conceptualisation of protection motivation theory. The key assumption of this theory, which is also espoused by the MPPACC, is that the perception of risks is a necessary but not a sufficient condition for adaptive behaviour (Grothmann & Patt, 2005). Rather, risk perception will only result in adaptive action when the indicators of the coping appraisal are also high, which are perceived self-efficacy, outcome efficacy, and adaptation costs (Grothmann & Patt, 2005). It is particularly when people perceive high self-efficacy, high outcome efficacy, and low adaptation costs that risk perception leads to behaviour (Bubeck, Botzen, & Aerts, 2012). In the following section, the indicators of the coping appraisal are defined and further discussed.

### 3.1.2 Self-efficacy

The coping appraisal partly depends on *self-efficacy*, referring to a person's perception of their own ability to engage in adaptive behaviour (Burnham & Ma, 2017). It is assumed that adaptive behaviour is more likely when people believe they are able to engage in the relevant behaviour. This hypothesis is supported by numerous studies (Arunrat, Wang, Pumijumnong, Sereenonchai, & Cai, 2017; Demuth, Morss, Lazo, & Trumbo, 2016; Gebrehiwot & van der Veen, 2015; W.-S. Hung et al., 2014; Kuruppu & Liverman, 2011; Martin, Bender, & Raish, 2007; McFarlane, McGee, & Faulkner, 2011; Ung, Luginaah, Chuenpagdee, & Campbell, 2016). For example, amongst Chinese farmers, self-efficacy was consistently found to be the best predictor of adaptive behaviour, compared to farm characteristics, indicators of financial resources, and other psychological variables such as risk perception (Burnham & Ma, 2017). Similarly, self-efficacy was the strongest predictor of adaptation to rising sea levels and flooding in Greece (Koerth, Jones, et al., 2013).

However, some studies do not find a significant relationship between self-efficacy and adaptation behaviour (Harries, 2012; Paton, Kelly, Burgelt, & Doherty, 2006; Roesch-McNally, Arbuckle, & Tyndall, 2017; Semenza et al., 2011; van Duinen et al., 2015). The occurrence of null findings has sometimes been attributed to the fact that some adaptive behaviours may be perceived as so easy to perform that all participants perceive their self-efficacy as high (Bubeck, Botzen, Kreibich, & Aerts, 2013; van Duinen et al., 2015). A lack of variance in a measure can lead to nonsignificant correlations.

One study reported a negative correlation between self-efficacy and information seeking (Paton et al., 2006), suggesting that people who feel more confident in their abilities do not perceive the need to gather additional information. Another study found that not only participants who were low in self-efficacy but also participants who were high in self-efficacy were less likely to report the intention to engage in adaptive behaviours (Richert et al., 2017). The authors suggest that this may be because those with high self-efficacy had already implemented many measures and may therefore be less likely to implement even more measures in the future. Overall, this finding suggests that there might be a curvilinear relationship between self-efficacy and adaptation behaviour, where a moderate level of self-efficacy is most predictive of the intention to engage in adaptation.

### *3.1.3 Outcome Efficacy*

*Outcome efficacy* is another important indicator of the coping appraisal and refers to people's perceptions of the effectiveness or utility of a measure or behaviour in protecting them from a climate-related hazard (Samaddar, Chatterjee, Misra, & Tatano, 2014). Believing that an action is effective in providing protection is expected to be an important predictor of behaviour, as it provides people with a rationale to undertake a particular action. The evidence generally supports the notion that a greater perceived outcome efficacy of actions is associated with engaging in more adaptation behaviour (Demuth et al., 2016; Deng, Wang, & Yousefpour, 2017; Gebrehiwot & van der Veen, 2015; Hall & Slothower, 2009; Khanal, Wilson, Hoang, & Lee, 2018; Martin et al., 2007; Paton, Bürgelt, & Prior, 2008; Samaddar et al., 2014; Terpstra & Lindell, 2012). For example, a study conducted in Poland found that higher outcome efficacy was related to more flood preparedness (Działek, Biernacki, Fiedeń, Listwan-Franczak, & Franczak, 2016). Similarly, a Dutch study found that outcome efficacy was associated with a stronger intention to prepare for flooding (Terpstra & Lindell, 2012). However, a sizeable number of studies fail to find a significant relationship between outcome efficacy and adaptation (Brenkert-Smith, Champ, & Flores, 2012; Brody, Highfield, Wilson, Lindell, & Blessing, 2017; Elrick-Barr et al., 2016; Esham & Garforth, 2013; McGee, 2005; Poussin et al., 2014; Richert et al., 2017), suggesting that there are some conditions under which outcome efficacy is not significantly associated with adaptation behaviour. It may be that in such cases a lack of perceived self-efficacy may weaken the relationship between outcome efficacy and adaptation.

Interestingly, outcome efficacy can play a role in determining which type of adaptive behaviour people will undertake. A study on flooding in the

Netherlands found that if people perceived measures to adjust to incoming water to be effective (e.g. moving expensive furniture upstairs), they were less likely to have the intention to engage in measures to prevent water from entering the home (e.g. placing sandbags in front of the door) (Zaalberg, Midden, Meijnders, & McCalley, 2009). This finding may have important implications for practice. Practitioners need to carefully consider which behaviours they want people to engage in, as promoting the efficacy of one action may reduce the extent to which people engage in other adaptive behaviours. Additionally, this study demonstrates the importance of assessing outcome efficacy for each individual behaviour that is being considered in the study.

Outcome efficacy is often found to be a stronger predictor of adaptive behaviour than self-efficacy. For example, a study in the Netherlands found that outcome efficacy, but not self-efficacy, consistently predicted flood-preparedness behaviour (Zaalberg et al., 2009). Similarly, outcome efficacy was a stronger predictor of adaptation to drought than self-efficacy (Gebrehiwot & van der Veen, 2015). Outcome efficacy, but not self-efficacy, also predicted willingness to adopt defensible space against wildfires (i.e. removing flammable materials and pruning foliage in a ten-metre circle around the house) and interest in a wildfire consultation and mitigation programme (Hall & Slothower, 2009). Overall, research suggests that outcome efficacy is a good predictor of adaptive behaviour in most circumstances.

### 3.1.4 Perceived Costs of Adaptation

*Perceived costs of adaptation* are a third indicator of the coping appraisal and refer to the costs that people perceive to be involved with taking adaptive actions. Many adaptive actions are associated with costs, either monetary or in terms of time/effort. Especially preventive adaptive actions, described earlier as structural actions taken before the onset of a climate-related hazard, may cost significant amounts of time and money. The purchase of insurance against climate-related hazards can also be associated with substantial monetary costs. For example, the average yearly homeowner insurance premium was $1,045 in California in 2017 (Woolfolk, 2018). Insurance premiums for climate-related hazards are also expected to increase as such hazards will occur more often due to climate change (Coleman, 2003). The perception of costs from adaptive actions may therefore be an important barrier to adaptive behaviour. Some studies indeed reveal that high perceived costs form a barrier to engaging in adaptation behaviour (Brody et al., 2017; Gebrehiwot & van der Veen, 2015;

Koerth, Jones, et al., 2013; Mankad, Greenhill, Tucker, & Tapsuwan, 2013; van Duinen et al., 2015). However, a similar number of studies have found that perceived costs were not associated with adaptive behaviour (Bubeck et al., 2013; Dickinson, Brenkert-Smith, Champ, & Flores, 2015; Hall & Slothower, 2009; Harries, 2012). One study showed that perceived costs reduced the purchase of flood insurance, but that perceived costs were not significantly related to other, lower-cost, adaptive measures, such as having an emergency kit or making a household plan in case of flooding (Terpstra & Lindell, 2012). Therefore, perceived costs may particularly affect adaptation when adaptive actions are relatively costly. Of the three indicators that form the coping appraisal, the perception of adaptation costs has been studied the least frequently. This may be because this component is not included in the original conceptualisation of protection motivation theory (Rogers, 1975).

### *3.1.5 Interactions between Risk Perception, Self-efficacy, and Outcome efficacy*

The MPPACC specifies that risk perception functions as a trigger to activate or initiate the indicators of the coping appraisal (Grothmann & Patt, 2005). However, there is no clear theory of how risk perception and the coping appraisal are related and together affect adaptation (see also Plotnikoff & Trinh, 2010). So far, only a few studies have attempted to examine how risk perception and the indicators of the coping appraisal are related (e.g. Zaalberg et al., 2009), and these studies have tested different models (see Figure 2). We discuss these models below.

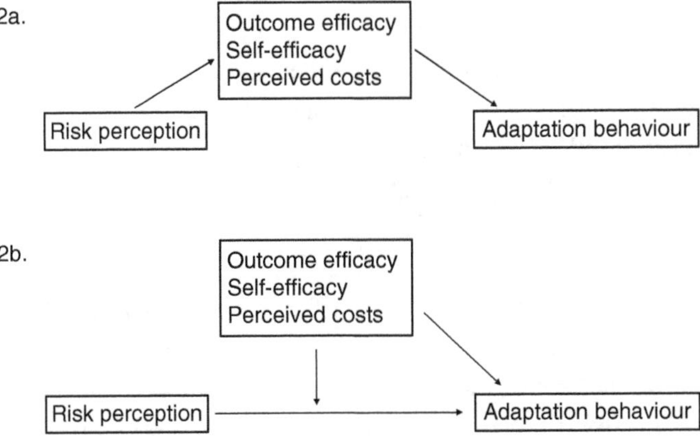


**Figure 2** Two ways to conceptualise the relationship between risk perception and the indicators of the coping appraisal. Figure 2a illustrates the mediation effect; Figure 2b illustrates the moderation effect.

First, the MPPACC may be interpreted as a mediation model, such that risk perception influences the indicators of the coping appraisal, which subsequently determine adaptive behaviour (see Figure 2a). This reasoning however was not supported in an empirical study conducted among Chinese farmers, which found no significant relationship between risk perception and self-efficacy, and the mediation effect was therefore not supported (Burnham & Ma, 2017). This may be attributable to the context in which the study was conducted. Specifically, the government played an important role in assisting farmers in the study area (Burnham & Ma, 2017). Therefore, farmers' self-efficacy levels may be lowered by this contextual variable, which could cause a floor effect that could explain why the mediation effect did not occur. Additionally, this study did not include the other two indicators of the coping appraisal (i.e. outcome efficacy and perceived costs). The question thus remains whether the mediation effect may appear between risk perception, adaptation behaviour, and either outcome efficacy or perceived costs.

The relationship between risk perception and the indicators of the coping appraisal can also be conceptualised as a moderation model, where both risk perception and the indicators of the coping appraisal independently influence adaptation behaviour, and that an interaction effect exists between them such that high risk perception combined with high levels of the coping appraisal indicators is most predictive of adaptation (see Figure 2b). Qualitative studies illustrate that low self-efficacy can indeed inhibit adaptive behaviour even when risk perception is high. Specifically, Swedish forest owners who acknowledged that climate change posed a risk to their forest but who had not yet implemented any adaptive measures often attributed their lack of adaptive action to a low sense of self-efficacy (Blennow & Persson, 2009). Similarly, while Irish participants who had experience Hurricane Charlie perceived high levels of risks from other hurricanes and flooding, this often did not translate into adaptive behaviour due to a lack of perceived self-efficacy (Fox-Rogers, Devitt, O'Neill, Brereton, & Clinch, 2016). These studies thus support the hypothesized interaction effect between risk perception and self-efficacy.

Yet, the moderation model received little support in quantitative studies. A study conducted amongst Sri Lankan farmers found that for three out of four adaptive behaviours,[2] no evidence of an interaction effect was found between risk perception and a combined self-efficacy/outcome efficacy measure (Truelove, Carrico, & Thabrew, 2015). Moreover, for one behaviour,

[2] The outcome variables were the intentions to engage in alternative crop selection, use of drought-resistant seeds, alternate wetting and drying, and the traditional communal cultivation technique called Bethma.

a reversed interaction effect was found: among farmers who perceived many risks, self-efficacy/outcome efficacy was only marginally related to adaptive behaviour, whereas for farmers low on risk perception, self-efficacy/outcome efficacy was strongly related to adaptive behaviour (Truelove et al., 2015). Similarly, no evidence of an interaction effect between risk perception, self-efficacy, and outcome efficacy was found in a study conducted among 752 flood-prone households in Germany for any of the four studied behaviours[3] (Bubeck et al., 2013). Out of twenty-four possible interaction effects, only one reached statistical significance, which likely occurred due to statistical chance. To conclude, the current evidence does not support different interpretations of how risk perception and the indicators of the coping appraisal may jointly influence adaptive behaviour. Risk perception and the indicators of the coping appraisal therefore likely independently influence adaptation behaviour.

## 3.2 Other Factors Specified in the MPPACC

In addition to the four factors described previously, which were directly drawn from the original protection motivation model, the MPPACC contains three more variables that extend the original protection motivation framework, namely experience with climate-related hazards, trust in government-issued adaptive measures, and perceived incentives to adapt. We elaborate on these variables next.

### *3.2.1 Experiences with Climate-related Hazards*

Together with risk perception, *experience with climate-related hazards* is the most frequently examined predictor of adaptive behaviour. Experiences are relevant for behaviour because they can shape our perception of situations and influence our judgements of outcomes (Cohen, Etner, & Jeleva, 2008; Wagar & Dixon, 2005). Studies have found that, in general, negative experiences motivate people to change their behaviour to avoid repetition of the experience, which is in line with operant conditioning (e.g. Haselhuhn, Pope, Schweitzer, & Fishman, 2012). Experiences with climate-related hazard may focus people's awareness on climate change and make the consequences of climate change more vivid and salient (Demski, Capstick, Pidgeon, Sposato, & Spence, 2017). For this reason, early research assumed that experience with climate-related hazards would be one of the primary motivators of adaptation

[3] The outcome variables were implementation of structural flood measures, flood-adapted building use, deployment of flood barriers, and the purchase of flood insurance.

(e.g. Laska, 1990). However, there are also theoretical reasons why experience could be negatively related to adaptation. For example, experiencing a climate-related hazard could lead people to believe they are able to cope with climate-related hazards and therefore do not need to prepare, especially if the experience was not strongly negative (Bihari & Ryan, 2012). Alternatively, people may become fatalistic following an encounter with a climate-related hazard, such that they believe that there is nothing they can do to protect themselves from climate-related impacts, which can inhibit adaptation (Ejeta, Ardalan, Paton, & Yaseri, 2018).

Mixed evidence regarding the relationship between experience and adaptation has been reported in the literature (Basolo et al., 2008). A wide variety of studies report that experience with climate-related hazards is associated with more adaptation behaviour (Aliagha et al., 2014; Baumann & Sims, 1978; Brenkert-Smith et al., 2012; Chatterjee & Mozumder, 2014; Coppock, 2011; Działek et al., 2016; Ejeta et al., 2018; Elrick-Barr et al., 2016; Ge, Peacock, & Lindell, 2011; Grothmann & Reusswig, 2006; Hamilton-Webb, Manning, Naylor, & Conway, 2016; Harries, 2012; Khanal et al., 2018; Lindell & Hwang, 2008; Osberghaus, 2015). One study found that the effects of experience with a climate-related hazard might even generalise beyond that specific hazard. Specifically, participants in the United Kingdom who had experienced wintertime flooding were more likely to report the intention to adapt to summertime heatwaves (Demski et al., 2017). However, there are also studies that fail to find a significant relationship between experience and adaptation (Chaney, Weaver, Youngblood, & Pitts, 2013; Deng et al., 2017; Fischer, 2011; Hasan, Ukkusuri, Gladwin, & Murray-Tuite, 2011; P. D. Howe, 2011; Joshi & Lalvani, 2010; Kellens, Zaalberg, & De Maeyer, 2012; Lo, 2013; Lo et al., 2015; Rincon, Linares, & Greenberg, 2001; Schulte & Miller, 2010). Moreover, a small number of studies reported that experience inhibited adaptation behaviour (Cahyanto et al., 2016; Hall & Slothower, 2009; Matyas et al., 2011). The mixed effects described in the quantitative studies previously cited were also found in a qualitative study conducted in Canada. This study found that the effect of experience with wildfires on adaptation differed from person to person. While most interviewees reported that their experience with wildfire motivated them to engage in more wildfire adaptation actions, some reported that the experience made them believe that undertaking preventive actions was pointless (McGee, McFarlane, & Varghese, 2009). This suggests that the effect of experience on adaptation behaviour is not uniform and likely differs from person to person. The question of which factors affect the strength and direction of this relationship remains unanswered.

It has also been suggested that the relationship between experience and adaptation may (partly) differ depending on the way in which experience with climate-related hazards is measured. Most studies rely on a simple yes-or-no question to assess whether participants have experienced a hazard (e.g. Deng et al., 2017; Faupel & Styles, 1993). Such yes-or-no measures have been criticized because they do not distinguish between different types of experiences and fail to capture the intensity of the experience (Demuth et al., 2016). Additionally, correlations based on dichotomized items can underestimate the strength of a relationship (MacCallum, Zhang, Preacher, & Rucker, 2002). Moreover, if many people report having an experience, there will be insufficient variance within the measure to detect a relationship with adaptive behaviour (Kanakis & McShane, 2016). Other studies have therefore measured the intensity of the experience by asking people whether they or close others experienced any physical damage, psychological distress, or financial damage (Demuth et al., 2016). The perceived intensity of the experience has been hypothesized to better predict adaptation than the self-reported presence (versus absence) of experience (Reynaud, Aubert, & Nguyen, 2013).

However, studies that have compared different measurements of experience have reported conflicting results. One study found that the severity of the experience, rather than its presence/absence, predicted adaptation to flooding (Laska, 1990). Yet, other studies could not replicate this effect. A study conducted in India found that only the experience of deaths in the respondent's community due to cyclones was predictive of evacuation behaviour, while individual experiences (measured both as the number of experiences and the severity of the experiences) did not predict evacuation behaviour (Sharma & Patt, 2012). This finding may be attributable to the collectivistic culture in which the study was conducted and the fact that the evacuation decision is usually a community decision in India (Sharma & Patt, 2012). A study conducted among Vietnamese households found that the presence/absence of experience did not predict any of the adaptive behaviours included in the study, whereas the intensity of the experience predicted only having a pumping set, but not whether participants had implemented floor elevations, had plans to move, or whether farmers used adaptive farming measures (Reynaud et al., 2013). Conversely, a study conducted in the Czech Republic found that both the yes-or-no measurement as well as the assessment of the intensity of the experience predicted adaptation to flooding (Stojanov, Duží, Daněk, Němec, & Procházka, 2015). The currently available evidence therefore suggests that the assessment of experience as either yes-or-no or the intensity of the experience cannot account for the divergent findings that have been reported in the literature. To conclude, we do note that the assessment of experience with evacuation has been consistently found to predict evacuation behaviour and future intentions to evacuate (Burnside, Miller, & Rivera, 2007; Demuth et al., 2016; Morss et al., 2016; Riad, Norris, & Ruback, 1999; Sadri, Ukkusuri, & Gladwin, 2017; Sharma & Patt, 2012). Experience can therefore also be assessed as previous experiences with adaptive behaviour.

Some other suggestions have been offered to explain under which conditions experience is likely to be related to adaptation behaviour, but they have not yet been investigated extensively. It may be that the relationship between experience and adaptation behaviour depends on the type of climate-related hazard that is being studied. For example, one study found that experiencing a wildfire was negatively associated with purchasing wildfire insurance (Gan, Jarrett, & Gaither, 2014). This negative relationship may be expected as experiencing a wildfire reduces the probability that another wildfire will occur again soon because the wildfire-prone vegetation needs time to regrow (Gan et al., 2014). Therefore, people might be less inclined to purchase insurance in the first years following a wildfire experience. This reduction in vulnerability after experiencing a wildfire does not apply to other climate-related hazards such as flooding. Therefore, the role of experience in adaptation may depend on the type of climate-related hazard that is examined.

Another unexplored explanation is the near-miss experience, referring to experiences in which there was a significant probability of being adversely affected, but due to luck this was avoided (Dillon, Tinsley, & Cronin, 2011). Near-miss experiences are hypothesised to reduce future adaptive behaviour as they may give people the idea that they are invulnerable to climate-related hazards (Dillon et al., 2011). Indeed, two studies have found that people who unnecessarily evacuated from a hurricane reported lower intentions to evacuate from the next hurricane threat (Huang, Lindell, Prater, Wu, & Siebeneck, 2012; Tinsley, Dillon, & Cronin, 2012). Imprecise yes-or-no measurements of experience may not be able to distinguish between participants who have really experienced a climate-related hazard and participants who experienced a near-miss. Accurately assessing the type of experience and ensuring that the experience was not a near miss may account for some of the divergent findings in the literature.

The MPPACC proposes that the influence of experience on adaptation behaviour is indirect, namely by increasing people's perceptions of risks (Grothmann & Patt, 2005; see Figure 1). Studies generally support the hypothesis that the effect of experience on adaptation behaviour is mediated by the perception of risks (Demuth et al., 2016; Harries, 2012; Lindell & Hwang, 2008; Zaalberg et al., 2009). Some other studies also found a positive correlation between risk perception and experience but did not assess whether risk perception mediated the relationship between experience and adaptation behaviour (Ejeta et al., 2018; Grothmann & Reusswig, 2006; Huang et al., 2012; Kanakis & McShane, 2016; Knocke & Kolivras, 2007; Lo, 2013; Mishra & Suar, 2007; Osberghaus, 2015). Yet, a positive correlation between risk perception and experience was not found in all research, as some studies reported null effects (Arlikatti, Lindell, Prater, & Zhang, 2006; Deng et al., 2017; Ge et al., 2011; P. D. Howe, 2011; Koerth, Vafeidis, Hinkel, & Sterr, 2013; Sattler, Kaiser, & Hittner, 2000). In sum, most evidence supports the proposition that experience with climate-related hazards influences adaptation indirectly by increasing people's perception of risks.

### 3.2.2 Trust in Government-issued Adaptive Measures

Large-scale measures implemented by governments, such as dykes and seawalls, play an important role in protecting people from climate-related hazards. While government-issued adaptive measures are indispensable, they can potentially have an important drawback. If people perceive that the government has undertaken measures against climate-related hazards, they may believe that individual adaptation actions are no longer required. This expectation that people will be less prepared if they trust more that government-issued adaptation measures will be effective is referred to as the 'levee-effect' (Anderson & Kjar, 2008). The empirical evidence however mostly does not support the levee-effect. While some studies find that higher *trust in government adaptation measures* reduces the likelihood that individuals engage in adaptive action (Grothmann & Reusswig, 2006; McNeill et al., 2013), most studies report a non-significant relationship (Aliagha et al., 2014; Aliagha, Mar Iman, Ali, Kamaruddin, & Ali, 2015; Baumann & Sims, 1978; Koerth, Vafeidis et al., 2013; Lazo et al., 2010; McGee, 2005; Terpstra, 2011). Therefore, trust in government measures likely does not undermine individual and household adaptation behaviour in most circumstances.

The relationship between trust in government measures and adaptation can also be positive. Two studies have found that trust in warning systems and information from the government was positively associated with evacuation behaviour (Lazo, Bostrom, Morss, Demuth, & Lazrus, 2015; Paul, 2012). These studies suggest that trust in government measures may be positively associated with adaptation when it concerns informative or non-structural measures rather than structural measures. This may be because informative or non-structural measures do not offer any protection themselves, as they merely inform people that adaptive actions are needed. Therefore, trusting in these measures does not take away people's perceived need to adapt but rather enforces it.

Similarly to experience with climate-related hazards, trust in government measures is hypothesised to indirectly influence adaptation behaviour by reducing people's perception of risks (Grothmann & Patt, 2005; see Figure 1). One study found that the negative effect of trust on adaptation intentions was indeed fully mediated by the perception of risks and negative affect, with risk perception accounting for approximately 80 per cent of this relationship (Terpstra, 2011). Some studies found that trust in flood protection measures reduced the perception of risks from flooding, but these studies did not test whether the perception of risks mediated the relationship between trust in government measures and adaptive behaviour (Grothmann & Reusswig, 2006; Koerth, Vafeidis et al., 2013). Similarly, trust in a wildfire warning system (McNeill et al., 2013) and firefighters (McFarlane et al., 2011) reduced the perception of risks from wildfires, but the mediation effect of risk perception between trust and adaptive behaviours was again not tested. Overall, these studies support the idea that trust in government measures may indirectly inhibit adaptive behaviour by reducing people's perception of risks.

### 3.2.3 Perceived Incentives to Adapt

*Perceived incentives to adapt* (e.g. tax exemptions, financial gains) are specified within the MPPACC as an additional factor that may cause people to consider adaptation along with the perception of risks. To our knowledge, only one study has examined the relationship between perceived incentives to adapt and adaptation behaviour. This study found that Vietnamese farmers were more likely to have the intention to engage in adaptive farming practices if they perceived that the government would support such a switch (Dang et al., 2014). However, the relationship was no longer significant in a multivariate analysis that also considered the influence of other variables from the MPPACC, such as risk perception and self-efficacy. Perceived incentives may therefore influence adaptive behaviour mainly indirectly. Notably, the MPPACC does not clearly define the concept of 'perceived incentives', which complicates accurately assessing it and which may explain why this variable has not yet been extensively studied. For example, social norms have also been mentioned as a form of perceived incentives (Grothmann & Patt, 2005). The role of social norms in adaptation behaviour is further discussed later.

## 3.3 Dang, Li, and Bruwer's Extended Version of the MPPACC

Dang, Li, and Bruwer (2012) proposed an extended version of the MPPACC to integrate different theoretical perspectives on adaptation behaviour. Specifically, this model was developed to explain why farmers engage in adaptive behaviour. Importantly, Dang, Li, and Bruwer (2012) proposed that the theory of planned behaviour (Ajzen, 1991) could offer important insights in explaining adaptation behaviour, as adaptation often consists of planned actions rather than more unconscious processes. They argued that the component of social norms from the theory of planned behaviour (referred to as 'subjective norm' within the theory) represented an important addition to the MPPACC. They further proposed to include three other variables from major psychological theories into the model: negative affect, climate change perceptions, and habits (see Figure 1). We discuss these four variables next.

### 3.3.1 Social Norms

*Social norms* refer to informal rules that govern people's behaviour (Bicchieri & Muldon, 2014). Two types of social norms can be distinguished. *Injunctive norms* refer to perceptions of what other people perceive as appropriate conduct (Cialdini, 2007) and form a component of the theory of planned behaviour (Ajzen, 1991). Injunctive norms can influence behaviour, as people are motivated to avoid the social sanctions that are associated with violating them, and to receive the social rewards associated with adhering to them (Cialdini et al., 2006). *Descriptive norms* refer to perceptions of what others are doing (Cialdini, Reno, & Kallgren, 1990). They can motivate behaviour as the actions of the majority signal what behaviour is likely most effective and feasible in a situation (Cialdini et al., 1990).

Empirical research supports the notion that social norms play a role in adaptation behaviour. First, multiple studies confirm that people are more likely to engage in adaptive behaviour when they perceive strong injunctive norms to do so (Arunrat et al., 2017; Bates et al., 2009; Dang et al., 2014; Lo, 2013; Lo & Chan, 2017; Lo et al., 2015; Mankad et al., 2013). Interestingly, one study found that injunctive norms were only predictive of adaptive behaviour for people who identified as community oriented, whereas they did not predict adaptive behaviour for those who identified as individualists (Bright & Burtz, 2006). This suggests that injunctive norms may be more influential for some people than others. Some injunctive norms can demotivate people to adapt. For example, the perception that family members would not approve of wildfire adaptation was negatively associated with engaging in wildfire adaptive action (McFarlane et al., 2011). The direction of the norms (i.e. whether adaptation behaviour is perceived as being encouraged or frowned upon by others) therefore matters. Injunctive norms have been found to mediate the relationship between risk perception and adaptation (Lo, 2013). This suggests that the perception of risks affects the strength of perceived injunctive norms, which in turn affect adaptive actions. Only one study that we know of found a non-significant relationship between injunctive norms and adaptive behaviour.

Specifically, a non-significant relationship was found between injunctive norms to protect the environment against wildfires and intentions to engage in environmental wildfire protection, but injunctive norms were significantly associated with intentions to protect one's own home against wildfires (Bates et al., 2009). Overall, evidence strongly supports the influence of injunctive norms on adaptive behaviour.

While descriptive norms have been examined to a lesser extent than injunctive norms, the evidence also supports their relevance for adaptive behaviour. For example, a study among Sri Lankan farmers found that if farmers perceived that other farmers were using a particular adaptive farming technique, they were more likely to report the intention to also adopt that technique (Truelove et al., 2015). Similarly, in Germany, homeowners who perceived that neighbours were implementing flood reduction measures were more likely to implement flood reduction measures themselves (Bubeck et al., 2013). The perceived behaviour of other community members influenced whether people had the intention to install rainwater tanks in response to drought (Mankad et al., 2013). Descriptive norms also affected whether people had flood insurance in an Australian study (Lo, 2013), and seeing other neighbours evacuating was an important predictor of evacuation behaviour (Huang et al., 2012; Stein, Dueñas-Osorio, & Subramanian, 2010). Finally, one study found that descriptive norms were an important predictor of perceived self-efficacy and outcome efficacy (Bubeck, Botzen, Laudan, Aerts, & Thieken, 2018). The indicators of the coping appraisal may therefore mediate the effect of social norms on behaviour. This is in line with the theoretical reasoning that descriptive norms influence behaviour because they inform people's perceptions of the effectiveness and feasibility of behaviour. Overall, these studies indicate that both injunctive and descriptive social norms play an important role in adaptive behaviour.

### 3.3.2 Negative Affect: Worry, Concern, and Fear

We have previously discussed the role of risk perception as a motivational factor for adaptive behaviour. Studies in risk perception have identified that in addition to the 'cognitive' perception of risks, such as the perceived probability and severity of a hazard, there is also an emotional component to risk perception, namely *negative affect*, that may motivate people to undertake adaptive actions (Sjöberg, 1998). The 'risk-as-feelings' hypothesis suggests that negative affect can even be more predictive of behaviour than the cognitive perception of risks (Loewenstein, Hsee, Weber, & Welch, 2001). However, protection motivation theory suggests that too strong negative emotions may also form a barrier to adaptive behaviour, as it may cause people to block out or ignore threatening information, especially when people perceive low self- or outcome efficacy (Ruiter, Kessels, Peters, & Kok, 2014). The three types of affective responses that have been most frequently assessed in response to climate-related hazards are worry, concern, and fear. We discuss here to what extent these emotional reactions are associated with adaptive behaviour.

The most widely studied variable is people's concern about climate change or climate-related hazards. Most studies confirm that higher concern increases the likelihood that people engage in adaptive behaviour (Aliagha et al., 2015; Demski et al., 2017; Deng et al., 2017; Fischer, 2011; Fischer, Kline, Ager, Charnley, & Olsen, 2014; Mozumder, Raheem, Talberth, & Berrens, 2008; Ray, Hughes, Konisky, & Kaylor, 2017). In one study, concern about the impacts of climate change was consistently the strongest predictor of support for adaptation policy across four European countries, next to other predictors such as attitudes (Hagen et al., 2016). However, a small number of studies found no significant correlation between concern and adaptive behaviour (Dascher, Kang, & Hustvedt, 2014; Hamilton-Webb et al., 2016; McGee, 2005; Schulte & Miller, 2010), and some studies reported mixed results, where concern predicted some, but not all adaptive behaviours assessed in the studies (Haden, Niles, Lubell, Perlman, & Jackson, 2012; Roesch-McNally et al., 2017).

The evidence to support the relevance of worry in climate change adaptation is mixed. Two studies reported that worry was positively correlated with adaptation behaviour (Ge et al., 2011; Miceli, Sotgiu, & Settanni, 2008). Yet, another two studies did not find a significant relationship (McNeill, Dunlop, Skinner, & Morrison, 2016; Richert et al., 2017). In a similar vein, two studies indicated that higher levels of fear encouraged adaptation behaviour (Nozawa, Watanabe, Katada, Minami, & Yamamoto, 2008; Zhang et al., 2017), whereas two studies did not find a significant correlation between fear and adaptation (Grothmann & Reusswig, 2006; McFarlane et al., 2011). One study found that fear was correlated with purchasing insurance, but not with checking a hazard map (Takao et al., 2004). Such a mixed picture is also obtained for studies that measured negative affect more generally (e.g. do you feel negatively about climate change?), where one study found that negative affect encouraged adaptation (Brügger et al., 2015), whereas another found no significant correlation (Sattler et al., 2000). Finally, some studies that measured a variety of different types of negative affect found that such a composite index generally was positively associated with adaptation (Demuth et al., 2016; Ejeta et al., 2018; Kerstholt, Duijnhoven, & Paton, 2017; Terpstra, 2011). Overall, there is relatively convincing evidence that concern is positively associated with adaptation, whereas the results pertaining to fear, worry, and general negative affect are less clear. Yet, no studies to our knowledge report a negative correlation between negative affect and adaptive behaviour. We therefore find no evidence for the proposition that negative affect inhibits adaptation, for example, by leading to denial of the problem. This aligns with a result of a review on the effect of fear appeals that also found that eliciting more negative affect was usually associated with more protective behaviour, instead of the hypothesized curvilinear effect where too much negative affect is negatively associated with protective behaviour (Ruiter, Abraham, & Kok, 2001).

One study has examined the effect of positive affect on adaptation. This study found that people who experienced positive affect about heat were less likely to take appropriate adaptive measures during a heatwave (Lefevre et al., 2015). Positive affect may therefore form a barrier to adaptation in some specific circumstances. We further discuss the role of positive affect when we discuss intervention studies in Section 4.

### 3.3.3 Climate Change Perceptions

*Climate change perceptions* refer to the way people understand climate change and what people perceive to be its essential components (Weber & Stern, 2011). Since climate change is the cause of the increase in climate-related hazards, it makes intuitive sense that people's belief in the reality of climate change and perceptions of its negative consequences could motivate adaptive behaviour. However, some have argued that people adapt in response to locally occurring circumstances, and it therefore may not matter whether or not they believe that a particular hazard is being caused by climate change (Brenkert-Smith, Meldrum, & Champ, 2015). Moreover, it has been argued that overly emphasizing the climate aspect of adaptation could even reduce people's intentions to adapt if they are sceptical of climate change (Hine et al., 2016).

Climate change perception is a multidimensional concept that is usually conceptualised to consist of people's perceptions of the reality, causes, and consequences of climate change (Guy, Kashima, Walker, & O'Neill, 2014; Heath & Gifford, 2006; Poortinga, Spence, Whitmarsh, Capstick, & Pidgeon, 2011). We discuss the evidence associated with climate change perceptions according to this distinction. First, most studies found that belief in the reality of climate change was not associated with adaptive behaviour (Brenkert-Smith et al., 2015; Deng et al., 2017; Shao et al., 2017), although some exceptions could be found (Bateman & O'Connor, 2016; García de Jalón, Iglesias, Quiroga, & Bardají, 2013). It is not surprising that belief in the reality of climate change hardly correlates with adaptation, as only a very small percentage of people still deny the existence of climate change (Steg, 2018). Therefore, a measure of climate change belief may not be very informative because there is not enough variance for a meaningful relationship to be found. However, studies that assessed people's scepticism regarding climate change, that is, the extent to which people were doubtful about the science surrounding climate change, have found that higher levels of scepticism are associated with lower adaptation behaviour and policy support (Bishop, 2013; Brügger et al., 2015). Thus, it may not be outright denial of climate change but rather more subtly expressed doubts about climate science that form a barrier to engaging in adaptive behaviour.

Only one study examined whether people's perceptions of the causes of climate change affected adaptation and found no significant correlation (Kreibich, 2011). People's perceptions of the consequences of climate change were usually more predictive of adaptation than belief in the reality of climate change. For example, perceptions that climate change would influence locally occurring climate-related hazards have been found to predict adaptation (Botzen et al., 2013; Botzen & van den Bergh, 2012; Elrick-Barr et al., 2016). Another study found that perceiving climate change as leading to more flooding was associated with undertaking some adaptive measures (i.e. safeguarding documents, protecting the building against inflowing water), but not others (e.g. collecting information, undertaking structural measures) (Kreibich, 2011). Yet, when the consequences would take place did not appear to matter. People who were concerned about climate change expressed support for climate change policies regardless of whether they perceived the consequences to occur in the far future or now (Singh et al., 2017). This finding was counterintuitive as it could be expected that people would be more motivated to adapt if climate change was perceived as close in time. Overall, we found that specific perceptions of the consequences of climate change were predictive of adaptive behaviour, while perceptions of the reality and causes of climate change were less consistently associated with adaptation.

Some studies on climate change perceptions focused on adaptive behaviour of farmers and found that relationship between climate change perceptions and adaptation was different for farmers compared to the general population. Farmers tended to be more sceptical of climate change than the general public (Chatrchyan et al., 2017; Doll, Petersen, & Bode, 2017). For example, only 55 per cent of Danish farmers and around 60 per cent of Welsh farmers somewhat or strongly agreed that the climate was changing (Hyland, Jones, Parkhill, Barnes, & Williams, 2016; Woods, Nielsen, Pedersen, & Kristofersson, 2017). In contrast, more than 90 per cent of the general population in Europe endorsed the reality of climate change (Steg, 2018).[4] Despite their general scepticism regarding (anthropogenic) climate change, farmers seemed to be open to the idea of adaptation. A qualitative study conducted in Montana demonstrated that it was particularly the farmers who were sceptical of anthropogenic climate change who undertook extra measures in anticipation of long-term drought (Yung, Phear, DuPont, Montag, & Murphy, 2015). This may explain why farmers' perceptions of the reality, causes, and consequences of climate change were generally not significantly related to their engagement in adaptive farming practices (Haden et al., 2012; Houser, 2016; Li, Juhász-Horváth, Harrison, Pintér, & Rounsevell, 2017; Mase, Gramig, & Prokopy, 2017; Mazur, Curtis, & Rogers, 2013). Two studies even found a negative correlation between climate change perceptions and adaptive farming (Burnham & Ma, 2017; Wheeler, Zuo, & Bjornlund, 2013). These non-significant findings may be attributed to the fact that farmers were used to adapting to changing environmental circumstances by the nature of their profession and were therefore more open to adaptation than the general public, independent of their climate change perceptions (Arbuckle, Morton, & Hobbs, 2015). Yet, some studies found that climate change perceptions did play a role in farmers' engagement in adaptive farming (Arbuckle, Prokopy, et al., 2013; Blennow & Persson, 2009; Blennow, Persson, Tomé, & Hanewinkel, 2012; Dang et al., 2014). Some studies reported mixed results where climate change perceptions were associated with some, but not all, adaptive behaviour assessed in these studies (Jianjun, Yiwei, Xiaomin, & Nam, 2015; Woods et al., 2017). Therefore, it is still unclear under which conditions farmers' climate change perceptions play a role in influencing adaptive behaviour.

### 3.3.4 Habits

*Habits* refer to behaviours that people perform without thinking (Verplanken, 2006). Because habits occur automatically and are hard to control, habitual behaviour is difficult to change and may therefore form a barrier to engaging in adaptive behaviour. To our knowledge, only one study has examined the relationships between habits and adaptive behaviour. Farmers who reported that their farming practices were more habitual were somewhat more likely to report the intention to engage in adaptive farming (Dang et al., 2014). This effect was however no longer significant in a multivariate analysis that also included other variables, such as perceived risk and the indicators of the coping

[4] Please note that the items used in these studies differed somewhat. Specifically, the studies by Hyland et al. (2016) and Woods et al. (2017) offered a middle response option (e.g. 'unsure'), whereas the study discussed in Steg (2018) does not, which may have influenced the results (see also Greenhill, Leviston, Leonard, & Walker, 2014).

appraisal. Hence, this study did not support the hypothesis that habits are an important barrier to adaptive behaviour. A possible explanation is that most adaptive behaviours are performed only once (e.g. purchasing insurance, installing hurricane shutters) and are therefore not dependent on habits, which per definition concern behaviours that happen on a frequent basis.

## 3.4 Additional Factors Not Included in the MPPACC and Its Extension

During our review of the literature, many variables came up that were not included in the MPPACC or its extension. Yet, these variables may still theoretically be related to adaptation. Next, we discuss four of these variables, namely, place attachment, trust in government, knowledge of climate change and adaptation, and perceived responsibility.

### *3.4.1 Place Attachment*

*Place attachment* refers to the emotional connection that people have to a place (Altman & Low, 1992). This connection can be to both the physical (e.g. nature, buildings, landscape) as well as the social features (e.g. neighbours, community, family) of a place (Hidalgo & Hernández, 2001). It can be theorised that place attachment may be both negatively and positively related to adaptive behaviour. On the one hand, residents with strong place attachment are more invested in their place of residence and thus have more to lose (Anton & Lawrence, 2016; Collins, 2008). Therefore, strongly attached people also have much more to gain from the effort of preparing for hazards, which implies that stronger place attachment could promote adaptive behaviour (Collins, 2008). It has also been proposed that those who are strongly place attached possess more resources to deal with climate-related hazards because they are more likely to be involved in the local community (Bihari & Ryan, 2012; Paton et al., 2008). Community involvement allows people to share practical information and provide social support for preparing for natural hazards and has therefore been found to be positively related to hazard preparedness (McGee & Russell, 2003; Tierney, Lindell, & Perry, 2001). On the other hand, it has been suggested that place attachment could cause a spatial optimism bias, that is, a tendency to underestimate the likelihood of negative events occurring to that location and to reduce the cognitive dissonance that is associated with living in a valued but simultaneously risky environment (Billig, 2006). As a result, place attachment could be associated with lowered levels of adaptation.

A recent review suggested that the evidence regarding the relationship between place attachment and hazard preparedness was mixed, with both positive and negative effects being reported in the literature (Bonaiuto, Alves, De Dominicis, & Petruccelli, 2016). Our literature review indicated that most studies found a positive correlation between place attachment and adaptive behaviour (Bihari & Ryan, 2012; Kakimoto, Fujimi, Yoshida, & Kim, 2016; Kanakis & McShane, 2016; Kim & Kang, 2010; Kyle, Theodori, Absher, & Jun, 2010; Madhuri, Tewari, & Bhowmick, 2015; Mishra, Mazumdar, & Suar, 2010; Paton et al., 2008). Some studies reported more mixed findings where place attachment was significantly related to some, but not all adaptive behaviours included in these studies (Prior & Eriksen, 2013; Truelove et al., 2015). Another study found that place attachment was associated with preparedness among rural residents, but not among residents living in the wildland-urban interface (Anton & Lawrence, 2016).

Place attachment may however form a barrier to adaptive behaviour under specific circumstances. First, place attachment can be an important factor inhibiting people from migrating from dangerous locations. For example, residents of the island state of Tuvalu were highly resistant to evacuation for rising sea levels because of their strong attachment to their home islands and the relaxed way of living associated with the culture on the islands (Mortreux & Barnett, 2009). Similarly, residents of a coastal community in Louisiana reported strong intentions to continue living there, despite the fact that this community was facing rapid land loss and flooding due to rising sea levels (Simms, 2017). This resistance to move was rooted in people's strong ties to the place, from which they derived a sense of historical continuity as well as an extensive social network and social identity (Simms, 2017).

Stronger place attachment may also result in less adaptive behaviour when there is an incongruence between the kind of place attachment and the type of adaptive behaviour that is being studied. Said differently, place attachment might become a barrier to preparation when there is a mismatch between the meaning or perception of a place that locals have and the actions that are required to prepare for natural hazards (Anton & Lawrence, 2016). For example, attachment to the natural environment was negatively associated with wildfire preparedness, because wildfire preparedness involves removing trees and altering natural elements to which people are emotionally attached (Brenkert–Smith, Champ, & Flores, 2006; McFarlane et al., 2011). In these cases, the meaning of a place as a natural, unspoiled, and organic whole can hinder the adoption of effective actions to reduce the risks of wildfires (Lohm & Davis, 2015).

Next, place attachment may be negatively associated with adaptation by weakening the relationship between other variables and adaptation. Specifically, a study conducted in Italy found a weak positive correlation between place attachment and the intention to enact flood preventive behaviours (De Dominicis, Fornara, Ganucci Cancellieri, Twigger-Ross, & Bonaiuto, 2015). However, this study also found that place attachment reduced the correlation between risk perception and adaptive behaviour, such that those who perceived risks of flooding but were not very place attached were more likely to report the intention to engage in flood prevention than people who were highly place attached (De Dominicis et al., 2015). Overall, the research suggested that place attachment was mostly positively associated with adaptation but could be negatively associated with adaptation under specific conditions.

### 3.4.2 Trust in Governments

We have previously discussed the role of people's trust in specific measures implemented by the government to reduce the risk of climate-related hazards. Trust may also be assessed as institutional trust, or people's general trust in government and the government's ability to cope with climate-related hazards (Kellens, Terpstra, & De Maeyer, 2013). *General trust in government* may be important if people are to engage in government-recommended adaptive actions, because trust may affect the likelihood that people will comply with suggestions from governmental institutions (Chanley, Rudolph, & Rahn, 2000).

Indeed, a number of studies found that general trust in government increased the likelihood that people would engage in adaptive behaviour (Koerth, Jones, et al., 2013; S. Lin, Shaw, & Ho, 2008; Lo et al., 2015; Scolobig, De Marchi, & Borga, 2012; Shao et al., 2017; Soane et al., 2010). Trust in government also predicted, as would be expected, support for adaptation policies (Hagen et al., 2016). However, another study found that it was trust in scientists, but not government, that predicted support for adaptation policies (Kettle & Dow, 2016). This finding may be explained by the fact that most of the participants in this study were government employees themselves, and trust in the government may therefore be a less relevant factor for these participants. One study found that trust positively predicted perceived preparedness and having a plan, but not having supplies or knowing how to shut off utilities to prepare for hurricanes (Basolo et al., 2008). Some studies found non-significant relationships between trust in government and adaptation behaviour (Absher & Vaske, 2011; Elrick-Barr et al., 2016; Kerstholt et al., 2017; Reynaud et al., 2013). Furthermore, two studies found a negative correlation between trust in government information and adaptive behaviour (Absher & Vaske, 2011; H.-C. Hung, 2009). Overall, the findings regarding the effect of trust in governments on adaptation behaviour are mixed.

### 3.4.3 Knowledge of Climate Change and Adaptation

Policymakers often assume that an important reason why people do not engage in adaptive behaviours is that they lack the necessary *knowledge* about climate change, climate-related hazards, or ways to adapt. The assumption that providing people with information will cause them to change their behaviour is referred to as the 'information-deficit' hypothesis (Fox-Rogers et al., 2016).

A distinction can be made between objective knowledge, that is, a person's actual level of knowledge, and subjective knowledge, a person's perceived knowledge level (Stoutenborough & Vedlitz, 2014). Studies generally report that objective knowledge is positively associated with adaptive behaviour (Akompab et al., 2013; Bates et al., 2009; Collins, 2008; Joshi & Lalvani, 2010), with some studies also reporting non-significant effects (Arimi, 2014; Fischer, 2011). Yet, under specific circumstances, objective knowledge may be negatively related to adaptation. For example, one study found that having more knowledge about hurricanes led to a lower intention to seek information about them (Cahyanto et al., 2016). This finding may be attributed to the fact that residents who are knowledgeable may believe that they do not need to seek more information because they know how to prepare for a hurricane. Another study found that objective knowledge about flooding was negatively associated with willingness to buy sandbags (Botzen et al., 2009): it is not clear why a negative correlation was observed in this study.

Similarly, studies that have assessed subjective knowledge generally found a positive correlation with adaptive behaviour (Gebrehiwot & van der Veen, 2015; Kellens et al., 2012; Martin et al., 2007; Mishra & Suar, 2007). Yet, a study conducted in Florida did not find a significant correlation between subjective knowledge and hurricane preparedness (Ge et al., 2011). A study conducted amongst Australian farmers found that subjective knowledge about climate change was significantly associated with five out of fourteen measured adaptive farming practices (Mazur et al., 2013). Based on the studies reported here, we cannot conclude whether subjective or objective knowledge is more predictive of adaptive behaviour. This is partly because subjective knowledge has been less extensively studied compared to objective knowledge. One study that measured a mix of subjective and objective knowledge found that it was significantly associated with the behaviour of saving water during a drought (Deng et al., 2017). Generally, these studies suggest that both objective and subjective knowledge are mostly positively associated with adaptive behaviour, but not always.

### 3.4.4 Responsibility

Governments have in recent decades shifted from a 'defence-focused' approach to disaster risk reduction towards an approach characterised by 'risk management' (O'Hare, White, & Connelly, 2016). The latter consists of a decentralised approach that moves the responsibility of risk management to multiple actors including local governments, local communities, and individual households (O'Hare et al., 2016). While there have been campaigns to make individuals aware of these shifting approaches in risk management, individuals may not be aware of the extent to which they are responsible for adaptation (J. Klein, Juhola, & Landauer, 2017). Additionally, people may not accept the responsibility to adapt. This may lead to a situation where most people perceive the government as responsible for adaptive measures, while the government is relying on individuals to take adaptive measures (Fox-Rogers et al., 2016). The perception of *personal responsibility* may therefore play an important role in explaining adaptation behaviour.

Studies indeed found that people who perceived a personal responsibility to adapt to climate change were more likely to engage in adaptive behaviour (McFarlane et al., 2011; McNeill et al., 2013; Mulilis, Duval, & Bovalino, 2000). Conversely, perceiving the government as responsible for adaptation was negatively associated with adaptation (Begg, Ueberham, Masson, & Kuhlicke, 2017; Botzen et al., 2009). A study in the United Kingdom found that perceiving the government as responsible was associated with lower investment in flood protection measures. However, those who perceived scientists to be responsible for preventing floods were more likely to have purchased flood protection measures (Soane et al., 2010). This study also found that experiencing a flood could reduce people's perceived responsibility to adapt. This suggests that people may relinquish their personal responsibility to adapt following an encounter with a hazard, indirectly offering some support for the hypothesis that people can become fatalistic as a consequence of experiencing a climate-related hazard. A number of studies did not find a significant correlation between perceived responsibility and adaptive behaviour (Bichard & Kazmierczak, 2012; Harries, 2012; McGee, 2005; Schulte & Miller, 2010; Terpstra & Gutteling, 2008). Perceived responsibility is therefore not predictive of adaptive behaviour in all circumstances.

Responsibility is somewhat differently related to policy support. Studies have found that both perceived personal responsibility (Bateman & O'Connor, 2016) and perceived responsibilities of other agencies, including the government (Hagen et al., 2016), were associated with more support for adaptation policies.

Most people perceive a shared responsibility between individuals and governments in reducing the impacts of flooding (Bichard & Kazmierczak, 2012). This has important implications and emphasises that a perceived responsibility of governments to adapt does not necessarily mean that the individual perceives no personal responsibility.

## 4 Interventions to Encourage Adaptation

The previous section revealed a wide array of predictive variables that play a role in adaptive behaviour. In this section, we show how interventions have targeted some of these variables to promote adaptive behaviour. Interventions are most effective if they target key psychological antecedents of the behaviour in question (Michie et al., 2018). Research has shown that campaigns that provide people with information on how to prepare for a natural hazard did not lead to more preparedness behaviour (Ballantyne, Paton, Johnston, Kozuch, & Daly, 2000; Paton et al., 2008). Targeting knowledge therefore does not appear to be sufficient to promote adaptation. We discuss three interventions that aimed to change adaptive behaviour by targeting other relevant antecedents of adaptation behaviour: changing people's risk and efficacy perceptions, perceived social norms, and feelings, respectively.

### 4.1 Motivating Flood-preparedness through Risk and Efficacy Messages

We have previously discussed that risk perception, self-efficacy, and outcome efficacy are relevant determinants of adaptation behaviour within the MPPACC model. As such, addressing these variables could promote adaptation behaviour. This reasoning was tested in a study conducted in the Netherlands (Kievik & Gutteling, 2011). The Netherlands is a low-lying country that is highly vulnerable to risks of rising sea levels. Dutch citizens are however not used to preparing for flooding themselves, as they rely on the dyke system implemented by the government (Terpstra & Gutteling, 2008). This study therefore aimed to promote flood preparedness amongst Dutch citizens by addressing their perception of risks from flooding and by increasing their perceived self-efficacy and outcome efficacy of taking flood preparedness measures.

In an experimental study, the level of risk of flooding was systematically varied by showing participants messages emphasising that they had either a very high risk of flooding (i.e. they were in the top 10 per cent of people at risk of flooding) or a very low flood risk (i.e. they were in the bottom 10 per cent of people at risk of flooding). Moreover, self- and outcome efficacy were manipulated through a text that described flood measures that people could implement and that stressed their ease and effectiveness (high efficacy condition) or that provided no extra information (control condition). After being exposed to both manipulations, participants reported their intention to seek information on flood risks and their intention to undertake precautionary measures against flooding. Additionally, participants' actual information-seeking behaviour was measured by assessing whether they chose to view websites related to flood preparedness or unrelated websites when asked to access one of four provided websites.

Participants who were in the high-risk or high-efficacy condition reported stronger intentions to seek information on flood preparedness, had stronger intentions to undertake precautionary measures, and were more likely to click on the flood-related links than participants who were in the low risk or control efficacy condition. Interestingly, no interaction effect was found between risk perception and efficacy for any of the outcome variables (i.e. intended information seeking, actual information seeking, and intentions to take precautionary measures). This finding is in line with our previous discussion on the relationship between risk perception and self-efficacy and outcome efficacy, which also showed that there is likely no interaction and that risk perception and efficacy perceptions are likely independently associated with adaptation behaviour. Overall, this study demonstrates how texts designed to highlight risks or self-efficacy or outcome efficacy can increase the likelihood that people engage in adaptive behaviour.

## 4.2 Social Norm Information to Increase Wildfire Preparedness

Howe, Boldero, McNeill, Vargas-Sáenz, and Handmer (2018) developed an intervention to increase people's wildfire evacuation planning by targeting social norms. This approach could be effective as we discussed that in the literature both descriptive and injunctive norms were consistently associated with adaptation behaviour. To develop an evacuation plan, people need to consider when the evacuation is initiated; how to evacuate from home, work, or other locations; how road closures and redirection of traffic may affect possible evacuation routes; and whether all family members agree with the plan. Residents in East Australia have on average completed only two out of these four actions (Howe et al., 2018). An intervention was therefore developed that aimed to increase preparedness levels, targeting people's perceptions of the injunctive and descriptive norms associated with wildfire evacuation planning.

First, a pilot study suggested that a combined injunctive and descriptive norm message would probably be most effective in promoting adaptive behaviour.

This intervention was next tested in an experimental study. Participants were randomly allocated to one of three conditions. In the first condition, they were provided with information, namely, the acronym LIVE[5] to help them remember the steps associated with making an evacuation plan. In the second condition, participants received this information as a well as a combined descriptive/injunctive norm message stating that most people had made an evacuation plan and that people should have an evacuation plan. The third condition was a control condition in which the participants saw neither the acronym nor the normative message. The combined descriptive/injunctive norms message significantly increased people's intention to prepare a wildfire evacuation plan compared to either the control condition or participants who received only information. Interestingly, after three weeks, preparedness levels were higher for all conditions than immediately after the intervention. However, the increase in preparedness compared to the first measurement was greatest in the group that received the descriptive/injunctive norm message, compared to the other two conditions. The descriptive/injunctive norm intervention was therefore successful in increasing people's intentions and actual behaviour of wildfire evacuating planning.

This intervention demonstrates that reading a short text containing a combined descriptive/injunctive norm, a relatively easy to administer intervention, can influence real-life adaptive behaviours. This intervention also showed that the combined descriptive/injunctive norm was more effective in increasing evacuation preparedness than the information condition in which people received information in the form of an acronym, which did not significantly differ from the control condition in promoting evacuation planning. This supports previous research that has found that providing people only with information on what they need to do to adapt, while intuitive, is not sufficient to promote adaptive behaviour. Targeting other antecedents of adaptive behaviour in addition to knowledge can therefore significantly increase the uptake of adaptive behaviour.

## 4.3 Countering Positive Affect with Negative Affect to Promote Heatwave Preparedness

People are motivated to avoid possible negative consequences. As such, reminding people of climate-related hazards could prompt them to undertake protective behaviour. Yet, in the case of heatwaves, reminding people of the hazard may not be sufficient to promote adaptive behaviour, as people do not

[5] LIVE stands for: Leave when? In agreement? Vehicles/transport sorted? Evacuation routes determined? These four steps represent the necessary components of a wildfire evacuation plan.

necessarily perceive heatwaves as negative, especially people living in colder climates such as Northern and Central Europe (Lefevre et al., 2015). For example, people may enjoy the prospect of swimming or sunbathing during a heatwave. They may be therefore less likely to interpret a heatwave as a risky event that requires a protective response. To address this challenge, Bruine de Bruin and colleagues (2016) developed an intervention aimed at overriding the influence of positive affect by explicitly reminding participants of negative affect associated with heatwaves. Reminding people of negative affect may also be effective in promoting adaptation to other hazards, as many studies have shown that negative affect predicted adaptation to a variety of natural hazards.

During the intervention, participants were asked to either recall the highest temperature experienced in the past summer, the most unpleasant temperature experienced, the combined highest/most unpleasant temperature experienced, or they received no recall instructions (control condition). Participants then reported their intention to engage in ten heat protection behaviours during the next summer (e.g. avoid excessive alcohol consumption, avoid extreme physical exertion, walk in the shade). Overall, participants who recalled the most unpleasant experienced temperature or the combined highest/most unpleasant temperature reported higher intentions to undertake heat protective behaviours than participants in the control condition.

This study demonstrated how interventions for heatwaves might require a reminder that high temperatures are not always enjoyable, and that adaptation can be promoted by reminding people of their previous (negative) experiences with climate-related hazards. Interestingly, it is often argued (based on protection motivation theory) that eliciting strong negative affect, in the absence of perceived self- and outcome efficacy, may not be an effective strategy to promote behaviour as people may shut down or tune out negative affect-arousing information when they believe they are not able to reduce the risks (Ruiter et al., 2014). The study we have just discussed however showed that a subtle negative affect manipulation could be used to effectively promote adaptation intentions, probably because in this particular study the adaptive behaviours were relatively easy (e.g. closing curtains), and hence, self-efficacy was likely to be high. This could explain why the negative affect manipulation positively influenced behavioural intentions in this study. This finding is in alignment with our previous discussion on negative affect, where we also did not find any evidence for a potential negative relationship between negative affect and adaptation behaviour. In conclusion, reminding people of past negative experiences with climate-related hazards may be an effective way to increase people's intentions to adapt.

## 5 Linking Climate Change Mitigation and Adaptation

An important question that remains to be answered is how climate change adaptation behaviour relates to climate change mitigation behaviour. Climate change mitigation refers to actions that are aimed at reducing the magnitude of climate change by lowering emissions of greenhouse gasses (IPCC, 2014b). Examples of mitigation actions include reducing car use, using less electricity, eating less meat, and recycling (i.e. behaviours that are also referred to as sustainable or pro-environmental). While climate change mitigation and adaptation are now recognised as two key pillars in our response to climate change, climate change adaptation was for a long time a 'taboo topic' within environmentalist circles (Pielke et al., 2007). The idea was that people might feel less concerned about climate change if they learned about the possibility to adapt to its consequences (Carrico, Truelove, Vandenbergh, & Dana, 2015). Therefore, it was feared that if people learned about climate change adaptation, they would lose interest in mitigating climate change and diminish their support for mitigation policies (Howell, Capstick, & Whitmarsh, 2016). However, recent findings in the literature suggest that this reasoning may not be correct. Experimental studies showed that learning about adaptation was not associated with reduced concern about climate change or lowered support for mitigation policies, as has been often feared (Carrico et al., 2015; Howell et al., 2016). One study found that participants who were primed to think about rising sea levels and adaptation in their local area reported a higher willingness to engage in mitigation behaviours than participants in the control condition (Evans, Milfont, & Lawrence, 2014). This finding suggests that providing people with adaptation information may even increase mitigation efforts. Moreover, a survey in Switzerland and Great Britain showed that adaptation and mitigation behaviours and support for adaptation and mitigation policies are strongly positively correlated (Brügger et al., 2015)

Two explanations have been offered to explain why mitigation and adaptation actions are related. First, learning about adaptation may serve as a reminder of the potential risks that climate change can cause, which can increase the awareness of climate change and elicit risk perception in response to climate change, leading to support for mitigating climate change as a strategy to avoid adaptation altogether (Carrico et al., 2015). However, an experimental study did not find strong evidence that receiving information about adaptation options increased people's risk perception of climate change (Carrico et al., 2015). Therefore, the idea that thinking about adaptation increases the perception of risks from climate change was not supported.

Alternatively, it has been suggested that people may support both adaptation and mitigation behaviours and policies for the same underlying reasons. Said differently, some variables may be related to both adaptation and mitigation behaviour. The most intuitive predictor of both adaptation and mitigation is people's perception of climate change. One study found that belief in the reality of climate change and its anthropogenic causes predicted support for both adaptation and mitigation policies (Bateman & O'Connor, 2016). Similarly, awareness of climate change was associated with willingness to pay for both flood protection measures and energy-saving measures (Bichard & Kazmierczak, 2012). Furthermore, farmers who endorsed the reality and anthropogenic nature of climate change and were concerned about the impacts of climate change were more likely to support both adaptation and mitigation actions (Arbuckle, Morton, & Hobbs, 2013; Arbuckle, Prokopy et al., 2013). In Australia, perceptions that climate change would affect environmental hazards influenced both mitigation and adaptation actions (Elrick-Barr et al., 2016). Risk perception of climate change also predicted support for both mitigation and adaptation policies and intentions to engage in both mitigation and adaptation behaviours (Brügger et al., 2015). Concern about climate change, trust in environmental organisations, self-reported knowledge of climate change, and perceived responsibility to address climate change also predicted support for both mitigation and adaptation policies across four European countries (Hagen et al., 2016).

Yet, one study found the opposite effect: Danish farmers who did not believe that extreme weather events would have negative consequences on their production were more likely to implement both mitigation and adaptation strategies (Jørgensen & Termansen, 2016). This study further found that belief in the anthropogenic nature of climate change predicted neither mitigation nor adaptation action. Another study found that farmers' perceived risk of climate change predicted support for adaptation, but not mitigation policies (Arbuckle et al., 2015). While these findings do not support the idea that mitigation and adaptation are predicted by the same variables, they do however fit with our previous discussion that showed that findings pertaining to climate change perceptions could differ for farmers compared to the general public.

Variables that are associated with climate change perceptions are likely also relevant predictors of both mitigation and adaptation. First, climate change perceptions are related to people's political orientations, which may influence the way in which they interpret climate-related information (Hornsey, Harris, Bain, & Fielding, 2016; Weber, 2010). Political orientation was indeed found to predict both mitigation and adaptation behaviour in the United States, with liberals being more likely than conservatives to support mitigation and adaptation (Bateman & O'Connor, 2016). Second, people's views about nature, which are associated with climate change perceptions (Hornsey et al., 2016), have also been associated with support for both mitigation and adaptation policies (Brügger et al., 2015). This suggests that people who perceive and are concerned about the fragility of nature are also more attentive to information about the dangers of climate change, prompting support for both mitigation and adaptation.

Experiences with climate-related hazards have also been associated with mitigation and adaptation. Having experienced an environmental hazard in the past predicted mitigation and adaptation actions in an Australian sample (Elrick-Barr et al., 2016). This study also found that risk perception of environmental hazards was a predictor of both mitigation and adaptation behaviour. This finding was replicated by a study in the United Kingdom that found that those who had experienced a flood were more likely to support mitigation policies and to report the intention to adapt to heatwaves (Demski et al., 2017).

Finally, some variables that are not directly related to climate change, climate change perceptions, or climate-related hazards may also be predictive of both adaptation and mitigation. For example, the tendency to plan ahead has been found to predict both mitigation and adaptation action (Elrick-Barr et al., 2016).

The literature we have just reviewed demonstrates how different psychological variables can be predictive of both mitigation and adaptation behaviour. The number of variables that have so far been examined in relation to both adaptation and mitigation simultaneously has however been limited, and many other variables may also be predictive of both mitigation and adaptation (Brügger et al., 2015). Importantly, many of the variables that we have discussed in our literature review have been found to be also of importance in the mitigation domain (e.g. Gifford & Nilsson, 2014; IPCC, 2018; Steg & Vlek, 2009). For example, self-efficacy is an important predictor of both mitigation (Estrada, Schultz, Silva-Send, & Boudrias, 2017; Lauren, Fielding, Smith, & Louis, 2016) and adaptation behaviour (Burnham & Ma, 2017). Similarly, social norms have been identified to be of importance in mitigation (Farrow, Grolleau, & Ibanez, 2017) and adaptation behaviour (Lo, 2013). As such, studies on mitigation behaviour may hold important insights for the literature on adaptation behaviour.

Yet, some variables may be better conceptualised as unique predictors of either mitigation or adaptation behaviour and may be more predictive of one type of response to climate change compared to another. For example, one study found that in multivariate analyses, perceived risk predicted mitigation, whereas adaptation was predicted by perceptions of having all the necessary information to prepare (Semenza et al., 2011). Another study found that perceived responsibility for either adaptation or mitigation predicted adaptation and mitigation best, respectively, when controlling for the other type of responsibility (Bateman & O'Connor, 2016). That is, perceived responsibility to mitigate predicted mitigation behaviour better than perceived responsibility to adapt, and vice versa, when both variables were directly compared. This area of research is thus still in need of further development, and more research is necessary to disentangle in which situations specific variables predict both adaptation and mitigation behaviour.

To conclude, despite their seemingly different objectives, namely preventing climate change versus protecting oneself against the impacts of climate change, mitigation and adaptation behaviour may depend on similar motivating factors. An integration of the mitigation literature with the adaptation literature may therefore be beneficial. For example, an integrated theoretical framework that can account for both adaptation and mitigation behaviour, and that distinguishes between common and unique predictors of adaptation and mitigation behaviour, would represent an important contribution to increasing the coherence of the psychological literature on behavioural responses to climate change. This integration may also have important practical implications, as interventions can have broader impacts if they target the mutual antecedents of both mitigation and adaptation actions.

# 6 Research Agenda

Our review provides some key insight into the drivers of adaptation behaviour. Yet, important questions remain that may be addressed to further increase our understanding of adaptation behaviour. Next we introduce a comprehensive research agenda on understanding climate change adaptation behaviour. We discuss five themes: theory, methodology, adaptive behaviours, generalisation to populations-locations-hazards, and integration with other disciplines.

## 6.1 Theory

We discussed the research on adaptation on the basis of two theoretical frameworks, namely the MPPACC (Grothmann & Patt, 2005) and an extension of this framework proposed by Dang, Li, and Bruwer (2012). However, many studies we have reviewed did not explicitly test these or other theoretical frameworks but were merely explorative and focused on a limited set of variables. To gain more comprehensive insights into adaptation behaviour, it is imperative that future research moves towards examining a wider range of theory-based factors that may influence adaptation behaviour and systematically test comprehensive theories to explain climate adaptation behaviour.

Notably, some predictors in the literature have been studied much more extensively than others. Specifically, we find that risk perception and experience have been studied by a large number of studies, whereas other predictor variables such as social norms have been studied to a far lesser extent. Yet, it appears that experience and risk perception are not necessarily the strongest or most reliable predictors of adaptation behaviour. Relying on a theoretical framework such as the MPPACC ensures that a wider scope of predictor variables is consistently included in studies.

Second, the relationships among predictor variables and their combined influence on adaptation have barely been studied. Yet, our literature review shows that the relationship between many predictors and adaptation behaviour is often inconsistent across studies, suggesting that the strength of these relationships likely depends on other psychological variables. For example, we have shown how the relationship between experience with climate-related hazards and adaptation may depend on risk perception. Similarly, perceived social norms may influence perceptions of self- and outcome efficacy. To fully understand adaptation behaviour, it is important to study how different variables influence and interact with one another in producing adaptive behaviour. Theoretical models can help to systematically develop and test such hypotheses regarding the combined influence of predictor variables on adaptive behaviour.

Third, clear definitions and associated conceptualisations for the key constructs in the literature are still lacking. For example, the construct of self-efficacy is sometimes used to refer to perceptions of personal ability; at other times, it refers to perceptions of the effectiveness of one's own actions. Furthermore, measures are sometimes confounded, for example, when the indicators of the coping appraisal are all assessed in one measure. Yet, self-efficacy, outcome efficacy, and perceptions of adaptation costs represent distinct constructs that can independently vary from one another, making it inappropriate to assess them as a single construct. Similarly, measures of risk perception sometimes include components of negative affect such as fear or anxiety. Confounding the measures makes it difficult to assess which component is predicting the outcome of interest, therefore making the findings much less informative and making it impossible to test theory-derived hypotheses. Moreover, the comparison and integration of findings across studies is complicated. The lack of clear definitions has hindered the development of validated measures to assess the constructs of interest. This harms the development of the literature as it becomes much more difficult to compare studies and determine whether some null findings may be attributable to the measurement tool that was used. To achieve an accumulation of knowledge in the literature, it is critical to develop and validate measures for each of the key psychological constructs within the literature.

We make two specific recommendations with regard to the theoretical development in the adaptation literature. First, while the MPPACC seems a useful theoretical framework to study adaptation behaviour, a re-specification of this model may be required. Notably, research suggests that neither a mediating nor a moderating relationship between risk perception and the indicators of the coping appraisal were supported. As the relationship between risk perception and the indicators of the coping appraisal represents a key assumption within MPPACC, a theoretical revision of the model seems required in which risk perception and the indicators of the coping appraisal are re-conceptualised as two processes that independently affect adaptive behaviour.

Moreover, our review suggests that the MPPACC can be expanded with additional variables that appeared to be relevant predictors of adaptive behaviour, such as place attachment, responsibility, trust in governments, and knowledge. Additionally, other variables that we did not discuss, as they have hardly been studied, could also be relevant predictors of adaptation behaviour, such as perceptions of the psychological distance of climate change or people's personal values. The climate change mitigation literature may serve as a source of inspiration in this regard, as we showed in the previous section that the drivers of mitigation and adaptation behaviour might be very similar. In expanding the MPPACC, authors need to explicitly specify the theoretical relationship between predictor variables in the model to fully capture the relationships between variables that are at play in adaptation behaviour.

Furthermore, we stress the importance of further theory-based research for the development and evaluation of the effects of interventions to promote adaptive behaviour. The interventions we discussed in this Element mostly targeted one or two key antecedent variables. Interventions that target multiple factors included in a relevant theoretical framework are likely more effective in promoting adaptation behaviour than interventions that focus on a single variable. Moreover, theory-based interventions can in turn inform theory building, as they offer an empirical test of the relationships specified in the model.

## 6.2 Methodology

Some methodological improvements can further advance the climate change adaptation literature. First, most studies reviewed here rely on cross-sectional correlational designs. While it is important to study adaptation in real-life situations, this method has some limitations. Typically, no clear conclusions can be drawn about the causality of relationships based on correlational research. Additionally, some relationships cannot be adequately studied in a cross-sectional design. For example, the relationship between risk perception and adaptation behaviour necessarily contains a cause-and-effect dynamic that cannot be easily captured in correlational research, because it requires the measurement of current levels of risk perception as well as future behaviours (Weinstein et al., 1998). It is therefore important to also use experimental and longitudinal designs to study the relationship between predictor variables and adaptation behaviour. Experimental studies enable control over possible confounds and allow us to firmly establish the causality of relationships, while longitudinal designs can be used to realistically assess the dynamic relationship between variables, in addition to establishing causality.

Second, more studies are needed that test different interventions to encourage adaptation behaviour. We have reviewed three studies that demonstrate how different antecedents of adaptive behaviour can be targeted to encourage adaptive behaviour. To our knowledge, these studies are the only intervention studies on adaptation published in peer-reviewed journals. More intervention studies are necessary to determine which strategies are most effective in promoting adaptive behaviour, and to determine whether the variables that are found to be predictive of adaptation behaviour are also practically relevant in influencing real-life behaviour. As such, intervention studies are key for informing practice and developing evidence-based interventions.

## 6.3 Adaptive Behaviours

In the introduction of this Element, we discussed a variety of outcome variables that are considered adaptive behaviour, such as evacuation, preparative behaviours, and purchasing insurance. The studies that we have reviewed have measured a wide variety of these different types of behaviours. In the interest of clarity, we discussed to what extent various variables were related to adaptation behaviour in general, and we did not discuss whether some variables might be more strongly related to some types of adaptation behaviours than to others. Yet, some evidence suggests that some variables may indeed be more predictive of some adaptive behaviour compared to others (Basolo et al., 2008; McNeill et al., 2013). Future research could therefore systematically examine whether the psychological variables discussed in this review can consistently predict different types of adaptation behaviour to the same extent, for example, by systematically comparing the importance of different psychological variables in predicting different adaptive behaviours. This would also address the issue that most of the studies we reviewed in this Element focused on preparative or protective actions, while other behaviours, such as policy support, have been studied to a lesser extent (see also Van Valkengoed & Steg, 2019).

An important related question is explaining how people choose between different types of adaptive behaviours when these behaviours are mutually exclusive. For example, both evacuation and staying and defending one's property are promoted as adaptive responses by the Australian government (Tibbits & Whittaker, 2007). A study conducted in Australia found that people who intended to evacuate perceived more risks from wildfire than those who intended to stay and defend their property (McLennan, Paton, & Beatson, 2015). Examining which factors explain when people engage in one adaptive behaviour over another may therefore also be an important avenue for future research.

We introduced an initial categorisation of different types of adaptive behaviour in the first section of this Element, which is based on the behaviours that have been studied thus far. This categorisation is not theory based and is therefore open to further improvement and refinement. Future research to develop a categorisation that is more strongly rooted in theory may be necessary. In this Element, we could not discuss some categories of adaptive behaviour as we found that there were hardly any studies on these topics. For example, very few studies have aimed to explain why people might engage in maladaptive behaviour, that is, behaviours that increase vulnerability to climate-related hazards, such as denial of the problem, fatalism, or behaviours that increase vulnerability to climate risks in the long term (for an exception, see Meinel & Höferl, 2017). Studying the drivers of maladaptation is important, as it predisposes people to the impacts of climate-related hazards. Moreover, it has been suggested that the factors influencing adaptation behaviour may differ from maladaptation behaviour (Paton et al., 2008). Maladaptation may therefore not merely represent the absence of adaptation but constitutes a distinct behavioural response that may be influenced by different variables and processes than adaptation behaviour (for an example outside the adaptation domain, see Kahlor, Olson, Markman, & Wang, 2018).

Furthermore, we focused on studies that have examined behavioural adaptation to climate change as an outcome. Yet, another important component of climate change adaptation is people's mental preparedness or psychological adaptation to climate change, referring to the way in which people cope with the anxiety and stress caused by the prospect of climate change and climate-related hazards (Helm, Pollitt, Barnett, Curran, & Craig, 2018). So far, only a limited number of studies have examined which factors are associated with mental preparedness to engage with climate change (Helm et al., 2018). Studying which factors determine mental adaptation is important, as people's mental preparedness will likely also determine their behavioural response to climate change (Hamilton & Kasser, 2009). Mental preparedness is therefore a likely prerequisite to successful behavioural adaptation to climate change and represents an important unexplored field of study.

Moreover, we have not included group-level or community responses in adapting to climate change. To illustrate, one of the studies we reviewed examined whether people were engaging in community-oriented actions to prepare for a hurricane, such as helping neighbours prepare or contacting close others during the hurricane to ensure their safety (Kim & Kang, 2010). Such group behaviours could be assessed more in future studies. As this topic specifically pertains to group behaviour, additional psychological theories and variables may be relevant. Specifically, theories of group dynamics and social identity may include important variables in this respect (for applications of these theories in the field of mitigation, see Bliuc et al., 2015; Fielding & Hornsey, 2016; Jans, Bouman, & Fielding, 2018).

## 6.4 Generalisability across Research Populations, Locations, and Hazards

Future research could study the extent to which the findings discussed here generalise across locations, populations, and hazard types. Most studies that we have reviewed were conducted in the United States and Australia, followed by Europe and East Asia. Almost no studies were conducted in the continents of Africa or South America. This is despite the fact that Africa and South America are highly vulnerable to the impacts of climate change (IPCC, 2014d). Therefore, more research on the drivers of adaptation behaviour is needed in developing countries. More generally, more cross-cultural research is needed. For example, Australia and the United States represent highly individualistic countries. It is therefore key to understand whether research findings from these countries will also be applicable in other countries with different cultural orientations (Paton, Okada, & Sagala, 2013). Community-level experiences, but not individual experiences, predicted adaptation behaviour for participants from the collectivistic country India (Sharma & Patt, 2012). Moreover, social norms have been found to be more predictive of behaviour in collectivistic compared to individualistic countries (Eom, Kim, Sherman, & Ishii, 2016). Cross-cultural research can thus offer important insights into the generalisability of adaptation behaviour research, which may have important practical implications for the deployment of interventions across different cultures. Comparative studies that directly compare findings from different countries are especially informative in this respect (see for example Paton et al., 2013).

We showed that findings might differ between farmers and the general public in our discussion on climate change perceptions. Hence, findings obtained from the general public are not necessarily applicable to all groups. Systematically investigating to what extent findings obtained from the general public are applicable to different groups and vice versa is therefore important.

Next, it is important to study whether predictors of adaptation vary across different types of climate-related hazards. Our review suggests that studies focused mostly on flooding, hurricanes, and wildfires, whereas other hazards such as drought and heatwaves have been studied to a far lesser extent. We have only sparingly found papers that looked at adaptation to climate-related hazards such as vector-borne diseases, land/mudslides, and flash flooding. Therefore, future studies could expand their scope and examine all types of climate-related hazards, including hazards that may not be immediately associated with climate change by the public, such as vector-borne diseases. Particularly, as the drivers of adaptation behaviour may differ across different hazards, it is important to conduct cross-hazard analyses, that is, to examine the drivers of adaptive behaviour across hazards and to compare whether some psychological variables may be more predictive of adaptation behaviour for some particular hazards compared to others.

Moreover, studies have so far looked mostly at adaptation to climate-related hazards that have already historically been occurring in that location, and that may increase in frequency or severity due to climate change. Yet, climate change will also cause climate-related hazards to 'migrate' into new territories that have not been exposed to such hazards in recent history, exposing many thousands or even millions of people to novel climate-related hazards. For example, malaria is expected to spread to more regions due to climate change (Caminade et al., 2014). Similarly, a potentially large risk for tropical cyclones has been identified for the Persian Gulf, an area where no tropical cyclones have ever been recorded (N. Lin & Emanuel, 2016). Adaptation to such 'novel' hazards may depend on distinct psychological processes, as people cannot rely on previous experiences or historical accounts of the hazard to motivate them to undertake adaptive actions. In such cases, people need to engage in anticipatory adaptation rather than reactive adaptation, and the findings discussed in this review may therefore not be applicable in such circumstances. Therefore, research on adaptation to novel climate-related hazards is urgently needed.

## 6.5 Integration with Other Disciplines

This Element focused on the role of individuals and households in adapting to climate change. In this context, the psychological literature is highly useful to explain and predict adaptive behaviours. Yet, there is of course only so much that individuals and households can do to protect themselves against the negative impacts of climate change. In many cases, individual behaviours will only be successful if more large-scale measures are also undertaken. In this respect, the role of other actors such as governments and companies is critical, but successful adaptation by governments and companies also depends on the behaviour of individuals and households. For example, policy-mandated evacuation is only effective to the extent that individuals accept and comply with the policy. Successful adaptation by households and individuals therefore depends on other actors and vice versa. An integration of the literature we discussed here into the broader climate change adaptation discourse is necessary.

A large body of literature on the governance aspects of climate change adaptation has not yet considered the role of individuals and households in adaptation (e.g. Amundsen, Berglund, & Westskogh, 2010; Bauer & Steurer, 2014; Moser & Ekstrom, 2010). The actions of individuals and households are however increasingly forming an important component of governments' adaptation strategies. Conversely, individuals and households can form a key barrier to successful governmental adaptation, and government policy can in turn reduce households' intentions to adapt (Wamsler & Brink, 2014). Successful adaptation will therefore be dependent on the synergy between governments and households.

There is also an extensive literature that has aimed to identify the determinants of adaptive capacity, or a system's objective capability of adapting to climate change (Engle, 2011). Such determinants may include availability of financial resources, access to education, and institutional structures that support or hinder adaptation (Yohe & Tol, 2002). These indicators of adaptive capacity may interact with the psychological variables described in this Element. For example, people who have lower incomes and therefore less available resources for adapting may perceive less self-efficacy to adapt. Studying how such structural barriers and psychological variables interact in adaptation may therefore be an interesting avenue for future research (see also Burnham & Ma, 2017, for an example).

## 6.6 Conclusion

In this Element, we have discussed the psychology of climate change adaptation. We started by defining adaptation as actions to reduce or avoid the negative impacts of climate-related hazards. We specifically focused on the adaptation actions of households and individuals, who represent an important but often overlooked group within the adaptation process. Individuals and households can generally engage in six types of adaptive actions, namely seeking information, preparing before a hazard, protecting themselves during a hazard, evacuating, purchasing insurance, and engaging in political actions.

We introduced the MPPACC and an extension of this model to examine which factors might predict adaptation behaviour. We reviewed the theoretical rationale and empirical evidence associated with the variables included in these models. We introduced four additional variables (responsibility, knowledge, place attachment, and general trust in governments) that have not yet been considered in the MPPACC or its extension, but that seem relevant to understand adaptation behaviour. Our review suggests that the variables social norms, concern, self-efficacy, and outcome efficacy are most consistently found to be related to engaging in climate change adaptation behaviour in general (see also Van Valkengoed & Steg, 2019). The evidence concerning the other variables is mostly mixed, and it is premature to make strong conclusive statements. It is therefore important to investigate under which conditions variables are more or less predictive of different types of adaptive behaviour.

Next, we discussed how the psychological literature could contribute to promoting real-life adaptation behaviour. Specifically, we reviewed three intervention studies that showed that strategies that target key antecedents could encourage people's engagement in adaptation behaviour. Simply providing people with information on how to prepare for climate-related hazards does not appear to be sufficient to promote adaptation behaviour.

We highlighted the potential overlap between the adaptation literature and the mitigation literature, that is focused on behaviours to reduce climate change through lowering greenhouse gas emissions. We indicated that some variables such as climate change perceptions, political orientation, and experiences with climate-related hazards might predict both adaptation and mitigation behaviour. This has important theoretical and practical consequences, as it implies that an integration of these two bodies of literature that have so far been separate may be possible. This could lead to a more efficient and holistic approach to studying behavioural responses to climate change, as well as the design of interventions aimed at promoting both mitigation and adaptation simultaneously.

In the research agenda, we highlighted five areas where the adaptation literature could potentially be improved. Most importantly, we stressed the need for more theory-based research that studies multiple predictor variables simultaneously, as well as the relationships between these predictors. Methodological improvements, studying different types of adaptive behaviours, testing the generalisability of research findings, and integration of the psychological adaptation literature with other disciplines can also contribute to further advancing the psychological adaptation literature.

Overall, we conclude that the psychological literature on adaptation is a quickly growing body of literature that enjoys contributions by a wide variety of experts from different fields, including psychologists, political scientists, social geographers, and anthropologists. While the literature that we have discussed already offers important insights into the psychology of adaptation, there are still frontiers to be addressed to further advance the literature. In doing so, we have no doubt that this research will offer an important contribution to the challenge of promoting climate adaptive behaviour and reducing the unavoidable negative consequences of climate change to human health and well-being.

# References

Absher, J. D., & Vaske, J. J. (2011). The role of trust in residents' fire wise actions. *International Journal of Wildland Fire*, *20*, 318–325. http://doi.org/10.1071/WF09049

Adger, W. N. (2001). Scales of governance and environmental justice for adaptation and mitigation of climate change. *Journal of International Development*, *13*, 921–931. http://doi.org/10.1002/jid.833

Adger, W. N., Arnell, N. W., & Tompkins, E. L. (2005). Successful adaptation to climate change across scales. *Global Environmental Change*, *15*, 77–86. http://doi.org/10.1016/j.gloenvcha.2004.12.005

Aerts, J. (2009). Adaptation costs in the Netherlands: Climate change and flood risk management. In M. Heinen (Ed.), *Climate Research Netherlands – Research Highlights* (pp. 34–36). Wageningen, the Netherlands: Climate Changes Spatial Planning and Knowledge for Climate. https://bit.ly/2ENIwkW

Ajzen, I. (1991). The Theory of Planned Behaviour. *Organizational Behavior and Human Decision Process*, *50*, 179–211.

Akompab, D. A., Bi, P., Williams, S., Grant, J., Walker, I. A., & Augoustinos, M. (2013). Heat waves and climate change: Applying the health belief model to identify predictors of risk perception and adaptive behaviours in Adelaide, Australia. *International Journal of Environmental Research and Public Health*, *10*(6), 2164–2184. http://doi.org/10.3390/ijerph10062164

Aliagha, U. G., Jin, T. E., Choong, W. W., Nadzri Jaafar, M., & Ali, H. M. (2014). Factors affecting flood insurance purchase in residential properties in Johor, Malaysia. *Natural Hazards and Earth System Sciences*, *14*, 3297–3310. http://doi.org/10.5194/nhess-14–3297-2014

Aliagha, U. G., Mar Iman, A. H., Ali, H. M., Kamaruddin, N., & Ali, K. N. (2015). Discriminant factors of flood insurance demand for flood-hit residential properties: A case for Malaysia. *Journal of Flood Risk Management*, *8*, 39–51. http://doi.org/10.1111/jfr3.12065

Altman, I., & Low, S. (1992). *Place Attachment*. New York: Plenum.

Amundsen, H., Berglund, F., & Westskog, H. (2010). Overcoming barriers to climate change adaptation – a question of multilevel governance? *Environment and Planning C: Government and Policy*, *28*, 276–289. http://doi.org/10.1068/c0941

Anderson, W., & Kjar, S. A. (2008). Hurricane Katrina and the levees: Taxation, calculation, and the matrix of capital. *International Journal of Social Economics*, *35*(8), 569–578. http://doi.org/10.1108/03068290810889198

Anton, C. E., & Lawrence, C. (2016). Does place attachment predict wildfire mitigation and preparedness? A comparison of wildland–urban interface and rural communities. *Environmental Management*, *57*, 148–162. http://doi.org/10.1007/s00267-015–0597-7

Arbuckle, J. G., Morton, L. W., & Hobbs, J. (2013). Farmer beliefs and concerns about climate change and attitudes toward adaptation and mitigation: Evidence from Iowa. *Climatic Change*, *118*(3–4), 551–563. http://doi.org/10.1007/s10584-013–0700-0

Arbuckle, J. G., Morton, L. W., & Hobbs, J. (2015). Understanding farmer perspectives on climate change adaptation and mitigation: The roles of trust in sources of climate information, climate change beliefs, and perceived risk. *Environment and Behavior*, *47*(2), 205–234. http://doi.org/10.1177/0013916513503832

Arbuckle, J. G., Prokopy, L. S., Haigh, T., Hobbs, J., Knoot, T., Knutson, C., … Widhalm, M. (2013). Climate change beliefs, concerns, and attitudes toward adaptation and mitigation among farmers in the Midwestern United States. *Climatic Change*, *117*(4), 943–950. http://doi.org/10.1007/s10584-013–0707-6

Arimi, K. S. (2014). Determinants of climate change adaptation strategies used by rice farmers in Southwestern Nigeria. *Journal of Agriculture and Rural Development in the Tropics and Subtropics*, *115*(2), 91–99. http://doi.org/10.1002/jsfa.6452

Arlikatti, S., Lindell, M. K., Prater, C. S., & Zhang, Y. (2006). Risk area accuracy and hurricane evacuation expectations of coastal residents. *Environment and Behavior*, *38*(2), 226–247. http://doi.org/10.1177/0013916505277603

Arunrat, N., Wang, C., Pumijumnong, N., Sereenonchai, S., & Cai, W. (2017). Farmers' intention and decision to adapt to climate change: A case study in the Yom and Nan basins, Phichit province of Thailand. *Journal of Cleaner Production*, *143*, 672–685. http://doi.org/10.1016/j.jclepro.2016.12.058

Baan, P. J. A., & Klijn, F. (2004). Flood risk perception and implications for flood risk management in the Netherlands. *International Journal of River Basin Management*, *2*(2), 113–122. http://doi.org/10.1080/15715124.2004.9635226

Bai, Y., Liu, Q., Chen, X., Gao, Y., Gong, H., Tan, X., … Liu, G. (2018). Protection motivation theory in predicting intention to receive cervical cancer screening in rural Chinese women. *Psycho-Oncology*, *27*, 442–449. http://doi.org/10.1002/pon.4510

Ballantyne, M., Paton, D., Johnston, D., Kozuch, M., & Daly, M. (2000). *Information on Volcanic and Earthquake Hazards: The Impact on Awareness and Preparation*. Lower Hutt, NZ: Institute of Geological & Nuclear Sciences Limited science report.

Barnett, J., & O'Neill, S. (2010). Maladaptation. *Global Environmental Change*, *20*, 211–213. http://doi.org/10.1016/j.gloenvcha.2009.11.004

Basolo, V., Steinberg, L. J., Burby, R. J., Levine, J., Cruz, A. M., & Huang, C. (2008). The effects of confidence in government and information on perceived and actual preparedness for disasters. *Environment and Behavior*, *41*(3), 338–364. http://doi.org/10.1177/0013916508317222

Bateman, T. S., & O'Connor, K. (2016). Felt responsibility and climate engagement: Distinguishing adaptation from mitigation. *Global Environmental Change*, *41*, 206–215. http://doi.org/10.1016/j.gloenvcha.2016.11.001

Bates, B. R., Quick, B. L., & Kloss, A. A. (2009). Antecedents of intention to help mitigate wildfire: Implications for campaigns promoting wildfire mitigation to the general public in the wildland-urban interface. *Safety Science*, *47*, 374–381. http://doi.org/10.1016/j.ssci.2008.06.002

Bauer, A., & Steurer, R. (2014). Multi-level governance of climate change adaptation through regional partnerships in Canada and England. *Geoforum*, *51*, 121–129. http://doi.org/10.1016/j.geoforum.2013.10.006

Baumann, D. D., & Sims, J. H. (1978). Flood insurance: Some determinants of adoption. *Economic Geography*, *54*(3), 189–196.

Begg, C., Ueberham, M., Masson, T., & Kuhlicke, C. (2017). Interactions between citizen responsibilization, flood experience and household resilience: Insights from the 2013 flood in Germany. *International Journal of Water Resources Development*, *33*(4), 591–608. http://doi.org/10.1080/07900627.2016.1200961

Bicchieri, C., & Muldon, R. (2014). Social norms. In E. N. Zalta (Ed.), *The Stanford Encyclopedia of Philosophy*. https://plato-stanford-edu.proxy-ub.rug.nl/entries/social-norms/

Bichard, E., & Kazmierczak, A. (2012). Are homeowners willing to adapt to and mitigate the effects of climate change? *Climatic Change*, *112*, 633–654. http://doi.org/10.1007/s10584-011–0257-8

Bihari, M., & Ryan, R. (2012). Influence of social capital on community preparedness for wildfires. *Landscape and Urban Planning*, *106*, 253–261. http://doi.org/10.1016/j.landurbplan.2012.03.011

Billig, M. (2006). Is my home my castle? Place attachment, risk perception, and religious faith. *Environment and Behavior*, *38*(2), 248–265. http://doi.org/10.1177/0013916505277608

Bishop, B. H. (2013). Drought and environmental opinion: A study of attitudes towards water policy. *Public Opinion Quarterly*, *77*(3), 798–810.

Black, R., Bennett, S. R. G., Thomas, S. M., & Beddington, J. R. (2011). Migration as adaptation. *Nature*, *478*, 447–449. http://doi.org/10.1038/478477a

Blennow, K., & Persson, J. (2009). Climate change: Motivation for taking measure to adapt. *Global Environmental Change*, *19*, 100–104. http://doi.org/10.1016/j.gloenvcha.2008.10.003

Blennow, K., Persson, J., Tomé, M., & Hanewinkel, M. (2012). Climate change: Believing and seeing implies adapting. *PLOS ONE*, *7*(11), e50182.

Bliuc, A. M., McGarty, C., Thomas, E. F., Lala, G., Berndsen, M., & Misajon, R. (2015). Public division about climate change rooted in conflicting socio-political identities. *Nature Climate Change*, *5*(3), 226–229. http://doi.org/10.1038/nclimate2507

Bonaiuto, M., Alves, S., De Dominicis, S., & Petruccelli, I. (2016). Place attachment and natural hazard risk: Research review and agenda. *Journal of Environmental Psychology*, *48*, 33–53. http://doi.org/10.1016/j.jenvp.2016.07.007

Botzen, W. J. W., Aerts, J. C. J. H., & van den Bergh, J. C. J. M. (2009). Willingness of homeowners to mitigate climate risk through insurance. *Ecological Economics*, *68*(8–9), 2265–2277. http://doi.org/10.1016/j.ecolecon.2009.02.019

Botzen, W. J. W., Aerts, J. C. J. H., & van den Bergh, J. C. J. M. (2013). Individual preferences for reducing flood risk to near zero through elevation. *Mitigation and Adaptation Strategies for Global Change*, *18*, 229–244. http://doi.org/10.1007/s11027-012–9359-5

Botzen, W. J. W., & van den Bergh, J. C. J. M. (2012). Risk attitudes to low-probability climate change risks: WTP for flood insurance. *Journal of Economic Behavior and Organization*, *82*, 151–166. http://doi.org/10.1016/j.jebo.2012.01.005

Breakwell, G. M. (2010). Models of risk construction: Some applications to climate change. *Wiley Interdisciplinary Reviews: Climate Change*, *1*, 857–870. http://doi.org/10.1002/wcc.74

Brenkert–Smith, H., Champ, P. A., & Flores, N. (2006). Insights into wildfire mitigation decisions among wildland–urban interface residents. *Society and Natural Resources*, *19*, 759–768. http://doi.org/10.1080/08941920600801207

Brenkert-Smith, H., Champ, P. A., & Flores, N. (2012). Trying not to get burned: Understanding homeowners' wildfire risk-mitigation behaviors. *Environmental Management*, *50*, 1139–1151. http://doi.org/10.1007/s00267-012–9949-8

Brenkert-Smith, H., Meldrum, J. R., & Champ, P. A. (2015). Climate change beliefs and hazard mitigation behaviors: Homeowners and wildfire risk. *Environmental Hazards*, *14*(4), 341–360. http://doi.org/10.1080/17477891.2015.1080656

Bright, A. D., & Burtz, R. T. (2006). Creating defensible space in the wildland-urban interface: The influence of values on perceptions and behavior. *Environmental Management*, *37*(2), 170–185. http://doi.org/10.1007/s00267-004-0342-0

Brody, S. D., Highfield, W. E., Wilson, M., Lindell, M. K., & Blessing, R. (2017). Understanding the motivations of coastal residents to voluntarily purchase federal flood insurance. *Journal of Risk Research*, *20*(6), 760–775. http://doi.org/10.1080/13669877.2015.1119179

Brügger, A., Morton, T. A., & Dessai, S. (2015). Hand in hand: Public endorsement of climate change mitigation and adaptation. *PLOS ONE*, *10*(4), e0124843. http://doi.org/10.1371/journal.pone.0124843

de Bruin, W. B., Lefevre, C. E., Taylor, A. L., Dessai, S., Fischhoff, B., & Kovats, S. (2016). Promoting protection against a threat that evokes positive affect: The case of heat waves in the United Kingdom. *Journal of Experimental Psychology: Applied*, *22*(3), 261–271. http://doi.org/10.1037/xap0000083

Bubeck, P., & Botzen, W. J. W. (2013). Response to "The necessity for longitudinal studies in risk perception research." *Risk Analysis*, *33*(5), 760–762. http://doi.org/10.1111/risa.12028

Bubeck, P., Botzen, W. J. W., & Aerts, J. C. J. H. (2012). A review of risk perceptions and other factors that influence flood mitigation behavior. *Risk Analysis*, *32*(9), 1481–1495. http://doi.org/10.1111/j.1539-6924.2011.01783.x

Bubeck, P., Botzen, W. J. W., Kreibich, H., & Aerts, J. C. J. H. (2013). Detailed insights into the influence of flood-coping appraisals on mitigation behaviour. *Global Environmental Change*, *23*, 1327–1338. http://doi.org/10.1016/j.gloenvcha.2013.05.009

Bubeck, P., Botzen, W. J. W., Laudan, J., Aerts, J. C. J. H., & Thieken, A. H. (2018). Insights into flood-coping appraisals of protection motivation theory: Empirical evidence from Germany and France. *Risk Analysis*, *38*(6), 1239–1257. http://doi.org/10.1111/risa.12938

Bubeck, P., Botzen, W. J. W., Suu, L. T. T., & Aerts, J. C. J. H. (2012). Do flood risk perceptions provide useful insights for flood risk management? Findings from central Vietnam. *Journal of Flood Risk Management*, *5*, 295–302. http://doi.org/10.1111/j.1753-318X.2012.01151.x

Bui, L., Mullan, B., & McCaffery, K. (2013). Protection motivation theory and physical activity in the general population: A systematic literature review. *Psychology, Health & Medicine*, *18*(5), 522–542. http://doi.org/10.1080/13548506.2012.749354

Burkett, M. (2011). In search of refuge: Pacific islands, climate-induced migration, and the legal frontier. *Asia Pacific Issues*, *98*, 1–8.

Burnham, M., & Ma, Z. (2017). Climate change adaptation: Factors influencing Chinese smallholder farmers' perceived self-efficacy and adaptation intent. *Regional Environmental Change*, *17*, 171–186. http://doi.org/10.1007/s10113-016–0975-6

Burnside, R., Miller, D. S., & Rivera, J. D. (2007). The impact of information and risk perception on the hurricane evacuation decision-making of greater New Orleans residents. *Sociological Spectrum*, *27*, 727–740. http://doi.org/10.1080/02732170701534226

Cahyanto, I., Pennington-Gray, L., Thapa, B., Srinivasan, S., Villegas, J., Matyas, C., & Kiousis, S. (2016). Predicting information seeking regarding hurricane evacuation in the destination. *Tourism Management*, *52*, 264–275. http://doi.org/10.1016/j.tourman.2015.06.014

Caminade, C., Kovats, S., Rocklov, J., Tompkins, A. M., Morse, A. P., Colón-González, F. J., … Lloyd, S. J. (2014). Impact of climate change on global malaria distribution. *Proceedings of the National Academy of Sciences*, *111*(9), 3286–3291. http://doi.org/10.1073/pnas.1302089111

Carrico, A. R., Truelove, H. B., Vandenbergh, M. P., & Dana, D. (2015). Does learning about climate change adaptation change support for mitigation? *Journal of Environmental Psychology*, *41*, 19–29. http://doi.org/10.1016/j.jenvp.2014.10.009

Chaney, P. L., Weaver, G. S., Youngblood, S. A., & Pitts, K. (2013). Household preparedness for tornado hazards: The 2011 disaster in DeKalb county, Alabama. *Weather, Climate, and Society*, *5*, 345–358. http://doi.org/10.1175/WCAS-D-12–00046.1

Chanley, V. A., Rudolph, T., & Rahn, W. M. (2000). The origins and consequences of public trust in government: A time series analysis. *Public Opinion Quarterly*, *64*(3), 239–256. http://doi.org/10.1086/317987

Chatrchyan, A. M., Erlebacher, R. C., Chaopricha, N. T., Chan, J., Tobin, D., & Allred, S. B. (2017). United States agricultural stakeholder views and decisions on climate change. *Wiley Interdisciplinary Reviews: Climate Change*, *8*, e469. http://doi.org/10.1002/wcc.469

Chatterjee, C., & Mozumder, P. (2014). Understanding household preferences for hurricane risk mitigation information: Evidence from survey responses. *Risk Analysis*, *34*(6), 984–996. http://doi.org/10.1111/risa.12196

Cialdini, R. B. (2007). Descriptive social norms as under appreciated sources of social control. *Psychometrika*, *72*(2), 263–268. http://doi.org/10.1007/s11336-005–1495-y

Cialdini, R. B., Demaine, L. J., Sagarin, B. J., Barrett, D. W., Rhoads, K., & Winter, P. L. (2006). Managing social norms for persuasive impact. *Social Influence*, *1*(1), 3–15. http://doi.org/10.1080/15534510500181459

Cialdini, R. B., Reno, R. R., & Kallgren, C. A. (1990). A focus theory of normative conduct: Recycling the concept of norms to reduce littering in public places. *Journal of Personality and Social Psychology, 58*(6), 1015–1026. http://doi.org/10.1037/0022–3514.58.6.1015

Cohen, M., Etner, J., & Jeleva, M. (2008). Dynamic decision making when risk perception depends on past experience. *Theory and Decision, 64*(2–3), 173–192. http://doi.org/10.1007/s11238-007–9061-3

Coleman, T. (2003). The *Impact of Climate Change on Insurance against Catastrophes*. Sydney: The Institute of Actuaries of Australia. www.actuaries.asn.au/Library/Events/Conventions/2003/1050 coleman7a.pdf

Collins, T. W. (2008). What influences hazard mitigation? Household decision making about wildfire risks in Arizona's White Mountains. *The Professional Geographer, 60*(4), 508–526. http://doi.org/10.1080/00330120802211737

Coppock, D. L. (2011). Ranching and multiyear drought in Utah: Production impacts, risk perceptions, and changes in preparedness. *Rangeland Ecology & Management, 64*, 607–618.

Dang, H. L., Li, E., & Bruwer, J. (2012). Understanding climate change adaptive behaviour of farmers: An integrated conceptual framework. *The International Journal of Climate Change: Impacts and Responses, 3*(2), 255–272. http://doi.org/10.18848/1835–7156/CGP/v03i02/37106

Dang, H. L., Li, E., Nuberg, I., & Bruwer, J. (2014). Understanding farmers' adaptation intention to climate change: A structural equation modelling study in the Mekong Delta, Vietnam. *Environmental Science & Policy, 41*, 11–22. http://doi.org/10.1016/j.envsci.2014.04.002

Dascher, E. D., Kang, J., & Hustvedt, G. (2014). Water sustainability: Environmental attitude, drought attitude and motivation. *International Journal of Consumer Studies, 38*, 467–474. http://doi.org/10.1111/ijcs.12104

De Dominicis, S., Fornara, F., Ganucci Cancellieri, U., Twigger-Ross, C., & Bonaiuto, M. (2015). We are at risk, and so what? Place attachment, environmental risk perceptions and preventive coping behaviours. *Journal of Environmental Psychology, 43*, 66–78. http://doi.org/10.1016/j.jenvp.2015.05.010

de Sherbinin, A., Castro, M., Gemenne, F., Cernea, M. M., Adamo, S., Fearnside, P. M., … Shi, G. (2011). Preparing for resettlement associated with climate change. *Science, 334*(6055), 456–457. http://doi.org/10.1126/science.1208821

DEFRA. (2013). *The National Adaptation Programme: Making the country resilient to a changing climate*. Department for Environment, Food &

Rural Affairs. https://assets.publishing.service.gov.uk/government/uploads/system/uploads/attachment_data/file/727259/pb13942-nap-20130701.pdf

Demski, C., Capstick, S., Pidgeon, N., Sposato, R. G., & Spence, A. (2017). Experience of extreme weather affects climate change mitigation and adaptation responses. *Climatic Change, 140*, 149–164. http://doi.org/10.1007/s10584-016–1837-4

Demuth, J. L., Morss, R. E., Lazo, J. K., & Trumbo, C. (2016). The effects of past hurricane experiences on evacuation intentions through risk perception and efficacy beliefs: A mediation analysis. *Weather, Climate, and Society, 8*, 327–344. http://doi.org/10.1175/WCAS-D-15–0074.1

Deng, Y., Wang, M., & Yousefpour, R. (2017). How do people's perceptions and climatic disaster experiences influence their daily behaviors regarding adaptation to climate change? – A case study among young generations. *Science of the Total Environment, 581–582*, 840–847. http://doi.org/10.1016/j.scitotenv.2017.01.022

Dickinson, K., Brenkert-Smith, H., Champ, P., & Flores, N. (2015). Catching fire? Social interactions, beliefs, and wildfire risk mitigation behaviors. *Society & Natural Resources, 28*, 807–824. http://doi.org/10.1080/08941920.2015.1037034

Dillon, R. L., Tinsley, C. H., & Cronin, M. (2011). Why near-miss events can decrease an individual's protective response to hurricanes. *Risk Analysis, 31* (3), 440–449. http://doi.org/10.1111/j.1539–6924.2010.01506.x

Doll, J. E., Petersen, B., & Bode, C. (2017). Skeptical but adapting: What Midwestern farmers say about climate change. *Weather, Climate, and Society, 9*, 739–751. http://doi.org/10.1175/WCAS-D-16–0110.1

Działek, J., Biernacki, W., Fiedeń, Ł., Listwan-Franczak, K., & Franczak, P. (2016). Universal or context-specific social vulnerability drivers – Understanding flood preparedness in southern Poland. *International Journal of Disaster Risk Reduction, 19*, 212–223. http://doi.org/10.1016/j.ijdrr.2016.08.002

Egli, T. (2002). *Non-Structural Flood Plain Management: Measures and their effectiveness*. International Commission for the Protection of the Rhine. www.iksr.org/fileadmin/user_upload/Dokumente_en/rz_iksr_engl.pdf

Ejeta, L. T., Ardalan, A., Paton, D., & Yaseri, M. (2016). Predictors of community preparedness for flood in Dire-Dawa town, Eastern Ethiopia: Applying adapted version of Health Belief Model. *International Journal of Disaster Risk Reduction, 19*, 341–354. http://doi.org/10.1016/j.ijdrr.2016.09.005

Ejeta, L. T., Ardalan, A., Paton, D., & Yaseri, M. (2018). Emotional and cognitive factors influencing flood preparedness in Dire Dawa town, Ethiopia. *Natural Hazards, 93*(2), 715–737. http://doi.org/10.1007/s11069-018–3321-0

Elrick-Barr, C. E., Smith, T. F., Preston, B. L., Thomsen, D. C., & Baum, S. (2016). How are coastal households responding to climate change? *Environmental Science & Policy, 63*, 177–186. http://doi.org/10.1016/j.envsci.2016.05.013

Engle, N. L. (2011). Adaptive capacity and its assessment. *Global Environmental Change, 21*(2), 647–656. http://doi.org/10.1016/j.gloenvcha.2011.01.019

Eom, K., Kim, H. S., Sherman, D. K., & Ishii, K. (2016). Cultural variability in the link between environmental concern and support for environmental action. *Psychological Science, 27*(10), 1331–1339.

Esham, M., & Garforth, C. (2013). Agricultural adaptation to climate change: Insights from a farming community in Sri Lanka. *Mitigation and Adaptation Strategies for Global Change, 18*, 535–549. http://doi.org/10.1007/s11027-012–9374-6

Estrada, M., Schultz, P. W., Silva-Send, N., & Boudrias, M. A. (2017). The role of social influences on pro-environment behaviors in the San Diego region. *Journal of Urban Health, 94*, 170–179. http://doi.org/10.1007/s11524-017–0139-0

Evans, L., Milfont, T. L., & Lawrence, J. (2014). Considering local adaptation increases willingness to mitigate. *Global Environmental Change, 25*, 69–75. http://doi.org/10.1016/j.gloenvcha.2013.12.013

Farrow, K., Grolleau, G., & Ibanez, L. (2017). Social norms and pro-environmental behavior: A review of the evidence. *Ecological Economics, 140*, 1–13. http://doi.org/10.1016/j.ecolecon.2017.04.017

Faupel, C. E., & Styles, S. P. (1993). Disaster education, household preparedness, and stress responses following Hurricane Hugo. *Environment and Behavior, 25*(2), 228–249.

Feng, X., Liu, M., Huo, X., & Ma, W. (2017). What motivates farmers' adaptation to climate change? The case of apple farmers of Shaanxi in China. *Sustainability, 9*, 519. http://doi.org/10.3390/su9040519

Ferrario, F., Beck, M. W., Storlazzi, C. D., Micheli, F., Shepard, C. C., & Airoldi, L. (2014). The effectiveness of coral reefs for coastal hazard risk reduction and adaptation. *Nature Communications, 5*, 3794. http://doi.org/10.1038/ncomms4794

Fielding, K. S., & Hornsey, M. J. (2016). A social identity analysis of climate change and environmental attitudes and behaviors: Insights and opportunities. *Frontiers in Psychology, 7*, 121. http://doi.org/10.3389/fpsyg.2016.00121

Fischer, A. P. (2011). Reducing hazardous fuels on nonindustrial private forests: Factors influencing landowner decisions. *Journal of Forestry, 109*(5), 260–266.

Fischer, A. P., Kline, J. D., Ager, A. A., Charnley, S., & Olsen, K. A. (2014). Objective and perceived wildfire risk and its influence on private forest landowners' fuel reduction activities in Oregon's (USA) ponderosa pine ecoregion. *International Journal of Wildland Fire*, *23*(1), 143–153. http://doi.org/10.1071/WF12164

Fox-Rogers, L., Devitt, C., O'Neill, E., Brereton, F., & Clinch, J. P. (2016). Is there really "nothing you can do"? Pathways to enhanced flood-risk preparedness. *Journal of Hydrology*, *543*, 330–343. http://doi.org/10.1016/j.jhydrol.2016.10.009

Gan, J., Jarrett, A., & Gaither, C. J. (2014). Wildfire risk adaptation: Propensity of forestland owners to purchase wildfire insurance in the southern United States. *Canadian Journal of Forest Research*, *44*, 1376–1382. http://doi.org/10.1139/cjfr-2014–0301

García de Jalón, S., Iglesias, A., Quiroga, S., & Bardají, I. (2013). Exploring public support for climate change adaptation policies in the Mediterranean region: A case study in Southern Spain. *Environmental Science & Policy*, *29*, 1–11. http://doi.org/10.1016/j.envsci.2013.01.010

Ge, Y., Peacock, W. G., & Lindell, M. K. (2011). Florida households' expected responses to hurricane hazard mitigation incentives. *Risk Analysis*, *31*(10), 1676–1691. http://doi.org/10.1111/j.1539–6924.2011.01606.x

Gebrehiwot, T., & van der Veen, A. (2015). Farmers prone to drought risk: Why some farmers undertake farm-level risk-reduction measures while others not? *Environmental Management*, *55*, 588–602. http://doi.org/10.1007/s00267-014–0415-7

Gifford, R., & Nilsson, A. (2014). Personal and social factors that influence pro-environmental concern and behaviour: A review. *International Journal of Psychology*, *49*(3), 141–157. http://doi.org/10.1002/ijop.12034

Greenhill, M., Leviston, Z., Leonard, R., & Walker, I. (2014). Assessing climate change beliefs: Response effects of question wording and response alternatives. *Public Understanding of Science*, *23*(8), 947–965. http://doi.org/10.1177/0963662513480117

Griffin, R. J., Yang, Z., Ellen, H. ter, Boerner, F., Ortiz, S., & Dunwoody, S. (2008). After the flood: Anger, attribution, and the seeking of information. *Science Communication*, *29*(3), 285–315. http://doi.org/10.1177/1075547007312309

Grothmann, T., & Patt, A. (2005). Adaptive capacity and human cognition: The process of individual adaptation to climate change. *Global Environmental Change*, *15*, 199–213. http://doi.org/10.1016/j.gloenvcha.2005.01.002

Grothmann, T., & Reusswig, F. (2006). People at risk of flooding: Why some residents take precautionary action while others do not. *Natural Hazards*, *38*, 101–120. http://doi.org/10.1007/s11069-005–8604-6

Guy, S., Kashima, Y., Walker, I., & O'Neill, S. (2014). Investigating the effects of knowledge and ideology on climate change beliefs. *European Journal of Social Psychology*, *44*, 421–429. http://doi.org/10.1002/ejsp.2039

Haden, V. R., Niles, M. T., Lubell, M., Perlman, J., & Jackson, L. E. (2012). Global and local concerns: What attitudes and beliefs motivate farmers to mitigate and adapt to climate change? *PLOS ONE*, *7*(12), e52882. http://doi.org/10.1371/journal.pone.0052882

Hagen, B., Middel, A., & Pijawka, D. (2016). European climate change perceptions: Public support for mitigation and adaptation policies. *Environmental Policy and Governance*, *26*, 170–183. http://doi.org/10.1002/eet.1701

Hall, T. E., & Slothower, M. (2009). Cognitive factors affecting homeowners' reactions to defensible space in the Oregon Coast Range. *Society and Natural Resources*, *22*, 95–110. http://doi.org/10.1080/08941920802392187

Hamilton, C., & Kasser, T. (2009). Psychological adaptation to the threats and stresses of a four-degree world. https://clivehamilton.com/wp-content/uploads/2014/06/Psychological-adaptation-to-a-four-degree-world-FINAL.pdf

Hamilton-Webb, A., Manning, L., Naylor, R., & Conway, J. (2016). The relationship between risk experience and risk response: A study of farmers and climate change. *Journal of Risk Research*, *20*(11), 1379–1393. http://doi.org/10.1080/13669877.2016.1153506

Harries, T. (2012). The anticipated emotional consequences of adaptive behaviour: Impacts on the take-up of household flood-protection measures. *Environment and Planning A*, *44*, 649–668. http://doi.org/10.1068/a43612

Hasan, S., Ukkusuri, S., Gladwin, H., & Murray-Tuite, P. (2011). Behavioral model to understand household-level hurricane evacuation decision making. *Journal of Transportation Engineering*, *137*(5), 341–348.

Haselhuhn, M. P., Pope, D. G., Schweitzer, M. E., & Fishman, P. (2012). The impact of personal experience on behavior: Evidence from video-rental fines. *Management Science*, *58*(1), 52–61. http://doi.org/10.1287/mnsc.1110.1367

Heath, Y., & Gifford, R. (2006). Free-market ideology and environmental degradation: The case of belief in global climate change. *Environment and Behavior*, *38*(1), 48–71. http://doi.org/10.1177/0013916505277998

Helm, S. V., Pollitt, A., Barnett, M. A., Curran, M. A., & Craig, Z. R. (2018). Differentiating environmental concern in the context of psychological adaption to climate change. *Global Environmental Change*, *48*, 158–167. http://doi.org/10.1016/j.gloenvcha.2017.11.012

Hidalgo, M. C., & Hernández, B. (2001). Place attachment: Conceptual and empirical questions. *Journal of Environmental Psychology*, *21*, 273–281. http://doi.org/10.1006/jevp.2001.0221

Hine, D. W., Phillips, W. J., Cooksey, R., Reser, J. P., Nunn, P., Marks, A. D. G., . . . Watt, S. E. (2016). Preaching to different choirs: How to motivate dismissive, uncommitted, and alarmed audiences to adapt to climate change? *Global Environmental Change*, *36*, 1–11. http://doi.org/10.1016/j.gloenvcha.2015.11.002

Horney, J. A., MacDonald, P. D. M., Van Willigen, M., Berke, P. R., & Kaufman, J. S. (2010). Individual actual or perceived property flood risk: Did it predict evacuation from hurricane Isabel in North Carolina, 2003? *Risk Analysis*, *30*(3), 501–511. http://doi.org/10.1111/j.1539–6924.2009.01341.x

Hornsey, M. J., Harris, E. A., Bain, P. G., & Fielding, K. S. (2016). Meta-analyses of the determinants and outcomes of belief in climate change. *Nature Climate Change*, *6*, 622–626. http://doi.org/10.1038/nclimate2943

Houser, M. (2016). Who framed climate change? Identifying the how and why of Iowa corn farmers' framing of climate change. *Sociologia Ruralis*, *58*, 40–62. http://doi.org/10.1111/soru.12136

Howe, P. D. (2011). Hurricane preparedness as anticipatory adaptation: A case study of community businesses. *Global Environmental Change*, *21*, 711–720. http://doi.org/10.1016/j.gloenvcha.2011.02.001

Howe, P. D. L., Boldero, J., McNeill, I. M., Vargas-Sáenz, A., & Handmer, J. (2018). Increasing preparedness for wildfires by informing residents of their community's social norms. *Natural Hazards Review*, *19*(2), 04017029. http://doi.org/10.1061/(ASCE)NH.1527–6996.0000279

Howell, R. A., Capstick, S., & Whitmarsh, L. (2016). Impacts of adaptation and responsibility framings on attitudes towards climate change mitigation. *Climatic Change*, *136*(3–4), 445–461. http://doi.org/10.1007/s10584-016–1627-z

Huang, S.-K., Lindell, M. K., Prater, C. S., Wu, H.-C., & Siebeneck, L. K. (2012). Household evacuation decision making in response to Hurricane Ike. *Natural Hazards Review*, *13*(4), 283–296.

Hung, H.-C. (2009). The attitude towards flood insurance purchase when respondents' preferences are uncertain: A fuzzy approach. *Journal of Risk Research*, *12*(2), 239–258. http://doi.org/10.1080/13669870802497702

Hung, W.-S., Hu, S. C., Hsu, Y.-C., Chen, K.-L., Chen, K.-H., Yu, M.-C., & Chen, K.-T. (2014). Factors affecting the use of anti-malaria preventive measures among Taiwan immigrants returning to malaria-endemic regions. *Travel Medicine and Infectious Disease*, *12*, 370–377. http://doi.org/10.1016/j.tmaid.2013.07.001

Hyland, J. J., Jones, D. L., Parkhill, K. A., Barnes, A. P., & Williams, A. P. (2016). Farmers' perceptions of climate change: Identifying types. *Agriculture and Human Values*, *33*(2), 323–339. http://doi.org/10.1007/s10460-015–9608-9

IPCC. (2014a). Adaptation needs and options. In C. B. Field, V. R. Barros, D. J. Dokken, K. J. Mach, M. D. Mastrandrea, T. E. Bilir, … L. L. White (Eds.), *Climate Change 2014: Impacts, Adaptation, and Vulnerability. Part A: Global and Sectoral Aspects. Contribution of Working Group II to the Fifth Assessment Report of the Intergovernmental Panel on Climate Change* (pp. 833–868). Cambridge and New York: Cambridge University Press.

IPCC. (2014b). Annex II: Glossary. In Core Writing Team, R. K. Pachauri, & L. A. Meyer (Eds.), *Climate Change 2014: Synthesis Report. Contribution of Working Groups I, II and III to the Fifth Assessment Report of the Intergovernmental Panel on Climate Change* (pp. 117–130). Geneva, Switzerland: IPCC.

IPCC. (2014c). *Climate Change 2014: Impacts, Adaptation, and Vulnerability. Part A: Global and Sectoral Aspects. Contribution of Working Group II to the Fifth Assessment Report of the Intergovernmental Panel on Climate Change*, C. B. Field, V. R. Barros, D. J. Dokken, K. J. Mach, M. D. Mastrandrea, T. E. Bilir, … L. L. White (Eds.). Cambridge and New York: Cambridge University Press.

IPCC. (2014d). *Climate Change 2014: Impacts, Adaptation, and Vulnerability. Part B: Regional Aspects. Contribution of Working Group II to the Fifth Assessment Report of the Intergovernmental Panel on Climate Change*, C. B. Field, V. R. Barros, D. J. Dokken, K. J. Mach, M. D. Mastrandrea, T. E. Bilir, … L. L. White (Eds.). Cambridge and New York: Cambridge University Press.

IPCC. (2018). Summary for Policymakers. In V. Masson-Delmotte, P. Zhai, H.-O. Pörtner, D. Roberts, J. Skea, P. R. Shukla, … T. Waterfieds (Eds.), *Global Warming of 1.5°C. An IPCC Special Report on the Impacts of Global Warming of 1.5°C above Pre-industrial Levels and Related Global Greenhouse Gas Emission Pathways, in the Context of Strengthening the Global Response to the Threat of Climate Change* . Geneva, Switzerland: World Meteorological Organization.

Jacobson, C., Crevello, S., Chea, C., & Jarihani, B. (2019). When is migration a maladaptive response to climate change? *Regional Environmental Change*, *191*(1), 101–112. http://doi.org/10.1007/s10113-018–1387-6

Jamero, M. L., Onuki, M., Esteban, M., Billones-Sensano, X. K., Tan, N., Nellas, A., … Valenzuela, V. P. (2017). Small-island communities in the Philippines prefer local measures to relocation in response to sea-level rise. *Nature Climate Change*, *7*, 581–586. http://doi.org/10.1038/nclimate3344

Jans, L., Bouman, T., & Fielding, K. (2018). A part of the energy "in crowd": Changing people's energy behavior via group-based approaches. *IEEE*

*Power & Energy Magazine*, *16*(1), 35–41. http://doi.org/10.1109/MPE.2017.2759883

Jianjun, J., Yiwei, G., Xiaomin, W., & Nam, P. K. (2015). Farmers' risk preferences and their climate change adaptation strategies in the Yongqiao District, China. *Land Use Policy*, *47*, 365–372. http://doi.org/10.1016/j.landusepol.2015.04.028

Jørgensen, S. L., & Termansen, M. (2016). Linking climate change perceptions to adaptation and mitigation action. *Climatic Change*, *138*, 283–296. http://doi.org/10.1007/s10584-016–1718-x

Joshi, M. S., & Lalvani, A. (2010). "Home from home": Risk perceptions, malaria and the use of chemoprophylaxis among UK South Asians. *Ethnicity & Health*, *15*(4), 365–375. http://doi.org/10.1080/13557851003729098

Kahlor, L. A., Olson, H. C., Markman, A. B., & Wang, W. (2018). Avoiding trouble: Exploring environmental risk information avoidance intentions. Environment and Behavior, 1–32. http://doi.org/10.1177/0013916518799149

Kakimoto, R., Fujimi, T., Yoshida, M., & Kim, H. (2016). Factors promoting and impeding precautionary evacuation behaviour. *International Journal of Urban Sciences*, *20*(S1), 25–37. http://doi.org/10.1080/12265934.2016.1185958

Kalkstein, A. J., & Sheridan, S. C. (2007). The social impacts of the heat-health watch/warning system in Phoenix, Arizona: Assessing the perceived risk and response of the public. *International Journal of Biometeorology*, *52*, 43–55. http://doi.org/10.1007/s00484-006–0073-4

Kanakis, K., & McShane, C. J. (2016). Preparing for disaster: Preparedness in a flood and cyclone prone community. *Australian Journal of Emergency Management*, *31*(2), 18–24.

Kellens, W., Terpstra, T., & De Maeyer, P. (2013). Perception and communication of flood risks: A systematic review of empirical research. *Risk Analysis*, *33*(1), 24–49. http://doi.org/10.1111/j.1539–6924.2012.01844.x

Kellens, W., Zaalberg, R., & De Maeyer, P. (2012). The informed society: An analysis of the public's information-seeking behavior regarding coastal flood risks. *Risk Analysis*, *32*(8), 1369–1381. http://doi.org/10.1111/j.1539–6924.2011.01743.x

Kerstholt, J., Duijnhoven, H., & Paton, D. (2017). Flooding in The Netherlands: How people's interpretation of personal, social and institutional resources influence flooding preparedness. *International Journal of Disaster Risk Reduction*, *24*, 52–57. http://doi.org/10.1016/j.ijdrr.2017.05.013

Kettle, N. P., & Dow, K. (2016). The role of perceived risk, uncertainty, and trust on coastal climate change adaptation planning. *Environment and Behavior*, *48*(4), 579–606.

Khanal, U., Wilson, C., Hoang, V.-N., & Lee, B. (2018). Farmers' adaptation to climate change, its determinants and impacts on rice yield in Nepal. *Ecological Economics*, *144*, 139–147. http://doi.org/10.1016/j.ecolecon.2017.08.006

Kievik, M., & Gutteling, J. M. (2011). Yes, we can: Motivate Dutch citizens to engage in self-protective behavior with regard to flood risks. *Natural Hazards*, *59*, 1475–1490. http://doi.org/10.1007/s11069-011–9845-1

Kim, Y.-C., & Kang, J. (2010). Communication, neighbourhood belonging and household hurricane preparedness. *Disasters*, *34*(2), 470–488. http://doi.org/10.1111/j.1467–7717.2009.01138.x

Kind, J. M. (2014). Economically efficient flood protection standards for the Netherlands. *Journal of Flood Risk Management*, *7*(2), 103–117. http://doi.org/10.1111/jfr3.12026

Klein, J., Juhola, S., & Landauer, M. (2017). Local authorities and the engagement of private actors in climate change adaptation. *Environment and Planning C: Politics and Space*, *35*(6), 1055–1074. http://doi.org/10.1177/0263774X16680819

Klein, R. J. T., Huq, S., Denton, F., Downing, T. E., Richels, R. G., Robinson, J. B., & Toth, F. L. (2007). Inter-relationships between adaptation and mitigation. *Climate Change 2007: Impacts, Adaptation and Vulnerability. Contribution of Working Group II to the Fourth Assessment Report of the Intergovernmental Panel on Climate Change*, pp. 745–777. http://doi.org/10.1007/s10584-015–1395-1

Knocke, E. T., & Kolivras, K. N. (2007). Flash flood awareness in southwest Virginia. *Risk Analysis*, *27*(1), 155–169. http://doi.org/10.1111/j.1539–6924.2006.00866.x

Koerth, J., Jones, N., Vafeidis, A. T., Dimitrakopoulos, P. G., Melliou, A., Chatzidimitriou, E., & Koukoulas, S. (2013). Household adaptation and intention to adapt to coastal flooding in the Axios – Loudias – Aliakmonas National Park, Greece. *Ocean and Coastal Management*, *82*, 43–50. http://doi.org/10.1016/j.ocecoaman.2013.05.008

Koerth, J., Vafeidis, A. T., Hinkel, J., & Sterr, H. (2013). What motivates coastal households to adapt pro-actively to sea-level rise and increasing flood risk? *Regional Environmental Change*, *13*, 897–909. http://doi.org/10.1007/s10113-012–0399-x

Kreibich, H. (2011). Do perceptions of climate change influence precautionary measures? *International Journal of Climate Change Strategies and Management*, *3*(2), 189–199. http://doi.org/10.1108/17568691111129011

Kreibich, H., Thieken, A. H., Petrow, T., Müller, M., & Merz, B. (2005). Flood loss reduction of private households due to building precautionary measures – lessons learned from the Elbe flood in August 2002. *Natural*

*Hazards and Earth System Science*, *5*, 117–126. http://doi.org/10.5194/nhess-5–117-2005

Kuruppu, N., & Liverman, D. (2011). Mental preparation for climate adaptation: The role of cognition and culture in enhancing adaptive capacity of water management in Kiribati. *Global Environmental Change*, *21*, 657–669. http://doi.org/10.1016/j.gloenvcha.2010.12.002

Kyle, G. T., Theodori, G. L., Absher, J. D., & Jun, J. (2010). The influence of home and community attachment on firewise behavior. *Society and Natural Resources*, *23*, 1075–1092. http://doi.org/10.1080/08941920902724974

Laska, S. B. (1990). Homeowner adaptation to flooding: An application of the general hazards coping theory. *Environment and Behavior*, *22*(3), 320–357.

Lauren, N., Fielding, K. S., Smith, L., & Louis, W. R. (2016). You did, so you can and you will: Self-efficacy as a mediator of spillover from easy to more difficult pro-environmental behaviour. *Journal of Environmental Psychology*, *48*, 191–199. http://doi.org/10.1016/j.jenvp.2016.10.004

Lazo, J. K., Bostrom, A., Morss, R. E., Demuth, J. L., & Lazrus, H. (2015). Factors affecting hurricane evacuation intentions. *Risk Analysis*, *35*(10), 1837–1857. http://doi.org/10.1111/risa.12407

Lazo, J. K., Waldman, D. M., Morrow, B. H., & Thacher, J. A. (2010). Household evacuation decision making and the benefits of improved hurricane forecasting: Developing a framework for assessment. *Weather and Forecasting*, *25*, 207–219. http://doi.org/10.1175/2009WAF2222310.1

Lefevre, C. E., de Bruin, W. B., Taylor, A. L., Dessai, S., Kovats, S., & Fischhoff, B. (2015). Heat protection behaviors and positive affect about heat during the 2013 heat wave in the United Kingdom. *Social Science & Medicine*, *128*, 282–289. http://doi.org/10.1016/j.socscimed.2015.01.029

Li, S., Juhász-Horváth, L., Harrison, P. A., Pintér, L., & Rounsevell, M. D. A. (2017). Relating farmer's perceptions of climate change risk to adaptation behaviour in Hungary. *Journal of Environmental Management*, *185*, 21–30. http://doi.org/10.1016/j.jenvman.2016.10.051

Lin, N., & Emanuel, K. (2016). Grey swan tropical cyclones. *Nature Climate Change*, *6*, 106–111. http://doi.org/10.1038/nclimate2777

Lin, S., Shaw, D., & Ho, M.-C. (2008). Why are flood and landslide victims less willing to take mitigation measures than the public? *Natural Hazards*, *44*, 305–314. http://doi.org/10.1007/s11069-007–9136-z

Lindell, M. K., & Hwang, S. N. (2008). Households' perceived personal risk and responses in a multihazard environment. *Risk Analysis*, *28*(2), 539–556. http://doi.org/10.1111/j.1539–6924.2008.01032.x

Liu, T., Xu, Y. J., Zhang, Y. H., Yan, Q. H., Song, X. L., Xie, H. Y., . . . Ma, W. J. (2013). Associations between risk perception, spontaneous adaptation behavior to heat waves and heatstroke in Guangdong province, China. *BMC Public Health*, *13*, 913. http://doi.org/10.1186/1471–2458-13–913

Lo, A. Y. (2013). The role of social norms in climate adaptation: Mediating risk perception and flood insurance purchase. *Global Environmental Change*, *23*, 1249–1257. http://doi.org/10.1016/j.gloenvcha.2013.07.019

Lo, A. Y., & Chan, F. (2017). Preparing for flooding in England and Wales: The role of risk perception and the social context in driving individual action. *Natural Hazards*, *88*, 367–387. http://doi.org/10.1007/s11069-017–2870-y

Lo, A. Y., Xu, B., Chan, F. K. S., & Su, R. (2015). Social capital and community preparation for urban flooding in China. *Applied Geography*, *64*, 1–11. http://doi.org/10.1016/j.apgeog.2015.08.003

Loewenstein, G. F., Hsee, C. K., Weber, E. U., & Welch, N. (2001). Risk as feelings. *Psychological Bulletin*, *127*(2), 267–286. http://doi.org/10.1037/0033–2909.127.2.267

Lohm, D., & Davis, M. (2015). Between bushfire risk and love of environment: Preparedness, precariousness and survival in the narratives of urban fringe dwellers in Australia. *Health, Risk & Society*, *17*(5–6), 404–419. http://doi.org/10.1080/13698575.2015.1109614

MacCallum, R. C., Zhang, S., Preacher, K. J., & Rucker, D. D. (2002). On the practice of dichotomization of quantitative variables. *Psychological Methods*, *7*(1), 19–40. http://doi.org/10.1037/1082-989X.7.1.19

Madhuri, Tewari, H. R., & Bhowmick, P. K. (2015). Ingenuity of skating on marshy land by tying a pot to the belly: Living with flood is a way of life. *Environment, Development and Sustainability*, *17*, 1287–1311. http://doi.org/10.1007/s10668-014–9605-y

Maldonado, J. K., Shearer, C., Bronen, R., Peterson, K., & Lazrus, H. (2013). The impact of climate change on tribal communities in the US: Displacement, relocation, and human rights. *Climatic Change*, *120*, 601–614. http://doi.org/10.1007/978–3-319–05266-3_8

Mankad, A., Greenhill, M., Tucker, D., & Tapsuwan, S. (2013). Motivational indicators of protective behaviour in response to urban water shortage threat. *Journal of Hydrology*, *491*, 100–107. http://doi.org/10.1016/j.jhydrol.2013.04.002

Martin, I. M., Bender, H., & Raish, C. (2007). What motivates individuals to protect themselves from risks: The case of wildland fires. *Risk Analysis*, *27*(4), 887–900. http://doi.org/10.1111/j.1539–6924.2007.00930.x

Mase, A. S., Gramig, B. M., & Prokopy, L. S. (2017). Climate change beliefs, risk perceptions, and adaptation behavior among Midwestern U.S. crop farmers. *Climate Risk Management*, *15*, 8–17. http://doi.org/10.1016/j.crm.2016.11.004

Matyas, C., Srinivasan, S., Cahyanto, I., Thapa, B., Pennington-Gray, L., & Villegas, J. (2011). Risk perception and evacuation decisions of Florida tourists under hurricane threats: A stated preference analysis. *Natural Hazards*, *59*, 871–890. http://doi.org/10.1007/s11069-011–9801-0

Mazur, N., Curtis, A., & Rogers, M. (2013). Do you see what I see? Rural landholders' belief in climate change. *Society and Natural Resources*, *26*, 75–85. http://doi.org/10.1080/08941920.2012.686650

McFarlane, B. L., McGee, T. K., & Faulkner, H. (2011). Complexity of homeowner wildfire risk mitigation: An integration of hazard theories. *International Journal of Wildland Fire*, *20*(8), 921–931. http://doi.org/10.1071/WF10096

McGee, T. K. (2005). Completion of recommended WUI fire mitigation measures within urban households in Edmonton, Canada. *Environmental Hazards*, *6*, 147–157. http://doi.org/10.1016/j.hazards.2006.05.002

McGee, T. K., McFarlane, B. L., & Varghese, J. (2009). An examination of the influence of hazard experience on wildfire risk perceptions and adoption of mitigation measures. *Society and Natural Resources*, *22*, 308–323. http://doi.org/10.1080/08941920801910765

McGee, T. K., & Russell, S. (2003). "It's just a natural way of life … " An investigation of wildfire preparedness in rural Australia. *Environmental Hazards*, *5*, 1–12. http://doi.org/10.1016/j.hazards.2003.04.001

McLeman, R., & Smit, B. (2006). Migration as an adaptation to climate change. *Climatic Change*, *76*, 31–53. http://doi.org/10.1007/s10584-005–9000-7

McLennan, J., Paton, D., & Beatson, R. (2015). Psychological differences between south-eastern Australian householders who intend to leave if threatened by a wildfire and those who intend to stay and defend. *International Journal of Disaster Risk Reduction*, *11*, 35–46. http://doi.org/10.1016/j.ijdrr.2014.11.008

McNeill, I. M., Dunlop, P. D., Heath, J. B., Skinner, T. C., & Morrison, D. L. (2013). Expecting the unexpected: Predicting physiological and psychological wildfire preparedness from perceived risk, responsibility, and obstacles. *Risk Analysis*, *33*(10), 1829–1843. http://doi.org/10.1111/risa.12037

McNeill, I. M., Dunlop, P. D., Skinner, T. C., & Morrison, D. L. (2016). Predicting risk-mitigating behaviors from indecisiveness and trait anxiety: Two cognitive pathways to task avoidance. *Journal of Personality*, *84*(1), 36–45. http://doi.org/10.1111/jopy.12135

Mechler, R., Linnerooth-Bayer, J., & Peppiatt, D. (2006). *Microinsurance for Natural Disaster Risks in Developing Countries: Benefits, Limitations And Viability*. Geneva and Laxenburg: ProVention and the International Institute for Applied Systems Analysis.

Meinel, U., & Höferl, K.-M. (2017). Non-adaptive behavior in the face of climate change: First insights from a behavioral perspective based on a case study among firm managers in alpine Austria. *Sustainability*, *9*, 1132. http://doi.org/10.3390/su9071132

Miceli, R., Sotgiu, I., & Settanni, M. (2008). Disaster preparedness and perception of flood risk: A study in an alpine valley in Italy. *Journal of Environmental Psychology*, *28*, 164–173. http://doi.org/10.1016/j.jenvp.2007.10.006

Michie, S., Carey, R. N., Johnston, M., Rothman, A. J., de Bruin, M., Kelly, M. P., & Connell, L. E. (2018). From theory-inspired to theory-based interventions: A protocol for developing and testing a methodology for linking behaviour change techniques to theoretical mechanisms of action. *Annals of Behavioral Medicine*, *52*, 501–512. http://doi.org/10.1007/s12160-016–9816-6

Mishra, S., Mazumdar, S., & Suar, D. (2010). Place attachment and flood preparedness. *Journal of Environmental Psychology*, *30*, 187–197. http://doi.org/10.1016/j.jenvp.2009.11.005

Mishra, S., & Suar, D. (2007). Do lessons people learn determine disaster cognition and preparedness? *Psychology and Developing Societies*, *19*(2), 143–159. http://doi.org/10.1177/097133360701900201

Morss, R. E., Demuth, J. L., Lazo, J. K., Dickinson, K., Lazrus, H., & Morrow, B. H. (2016). Understanding public hurricane evacuation decisions and responses to forecast and warning messages. *Weather and Forecasting*, *31*, 395–417. http://doi.org/10.1175/WAF-D-15–0066.1

Mortreux, C., & Barnett, J. (2009). Climate change, migration and adaptation in Funafuti, Tuvalu. *Global Environmental Change*, *19*, 105–112. http://doi.org/10.1016/j.gloenvcha.2008.09.006

Moser, S. C., & Ekstrom, J. A. (2010). A framework to diagnose barriers to climate change adaptation. *Proceedings of the National Academy of Sciences*, *107*(51), 22026–22031. http://doi.org/10.1073/pnas

Mozumder, P., Raheem, N., Talberth, J., & Berrens, R. P. (2008). Investigating intended evacuation from wildfires in the wildland-urban interface: Application of a bivariate probit model. *Forest Policy and Economics*, *10*, 415–423. http://doi.org/10.1016/j.forpol.2008.02.002

Mulilis, J. P., Duval, T. S., & Bovalino, K. (2000). Tornado preparedness of students, nonstudent renters, and nonstudent owners: Issues of PrE theory. *Journal of Applied Social Psychology*, *30*(6), 1310–1329. http://doi.org/10.1111/j.1559–1816.2000.tb02522.x

Nozawa, M., Watanabe, T., Katada, N., Minami, H., & Yamamoto, A. (2008). Residents' awareness and behaviour regarding typhoon evacuation advice in Hyogo Prefecture, Japan. *International Nursing Review*, *55*(1), 20–26. http://doi.org/10.1111/j.1466–7657.2007.00589.x

O'Hare, P., White, I., & Connelly, A. (2016). Insurance as maladaptation: Resilience and the 'business as usual' paradox. *Environment and Planning C: Government and Policy, 34*(6), 1175–1193. http://doi.org/10.1177/0263774X15602022

Osberghaus, D. (2015). The determinants of private flood mitigation measures in Germany – Evidence from a nationwide survey. *Ecological Economics, 110*, 36–50. http://doi.org/10.1016/j.ecolecon.2014.12.010

Paek, H.-J., & Hove, T. (2017). Risk perceptions and risk characteristics. *Oxford Research Encyclopedia of Communication*. http://doi.org/10.1093/acrefore/9780190228613.013.283

Paton, D., Bürgelt, P. T., & Prior, T. (2008). Living with bushfire risk: Social and environmental influences on preparedness. *The Australian Journal of Emergency Management, 23*(3), 41–48.

Paton, D., Kelly, G., Burgelt, P. T., & Doherty, M. (2006). Preparing for bushfires: Understanding intentions. *Disaster Prevention and Management, 15*(4), 566–575. http://doi.org/10.1108/09653560610685893

Paton, D., Okada, N., & Sagala, S. (2013). Understanding preparedness for natural hazards: A cross cultural comparison. *Journal of Integrated Disaster Risk Management, 3*(1), 18–35. http://doi.org/10.5595/idrim.2013.0051

Paul, B. K. (2012). Factors affecting evacuation behavior: The case of 2007 cyclone Sidr, Bangladesh. *The Professional Geographer, 64*(3), 401–414. http://doi.org/10.1080/00330124.2011.609780

Pielke, R. J., Prins, G., Rayner, P., & Sarewitz, D. (2007). Lifting the taboo on adaptation. *Nature, 445*, 597–598. http://doi.org/10.1038/445597a

Plotnikoff, R. C., & Trinh, L. (2010). Protection motivation theory: Is this a worthwhile theory for physical activity promotion? *Exercise and Sport Sciences Reviews, 38*(2), 91–98. http://doi.org/10.1097/JES.0b013e3181d49612

Poortinga, W., Spence, A., Whitmarsh, L., Capstick, S., & Pidgeon, N. F. (2011). Uncertain climate: An investigation into public scepticism about anthropogenic climate change. *Global Environmental Change, 21*, 1015–1024. http://doi.org/10.1016/j.gloenvcha.2011.03.001

Porter, J. J., Dessai, S., & Tompkins, E. L. (2014). What do we know about UK household adaptation to climate change? A systematic review. *Climatic Change, 127*, 371–379. http://doi.org/10.1007/s10584-014–1252-7

Poussin, J. K., Botzen, W. J. W., & Aerts, J. C. J. H. (2014). Factors of influence on flood damage mitigation behaviour by households. *Environmental Science & Policy, 40*, 69–77. http://doi.org/10.1016/j.envsci.2014.01.013

Price, L. J., McFarlane, B., & Lantz, V. (2016). Wildfire risk mitigation and recreational property owners in Cypress Hills Interprovincial Park–Alberta. *Forestry Chronicle, 92*(1), 66–76. http://doi.org/10.5558/tfc2016-019

Prior, T., & Eriksen, C. (2013). Wildfire preparedness, community cohesion and social-ecological systems. *Global Environmental Change, 23*, 1575–1586. http://doi.org/10.1016/j.gloenvcha.2013.09.016

Rauf, S., Bakhsh, K., Abbas, A., Hassan, S., Ali, A., & Kächele, H. (2017). How hard they hit? Perception, adaptation and public health implications of heat waves in urban and peri-urban Pakistan. *Environmental Science and Pollution Research, 24*, 10630–10639. http://doi.org/10.1007/s11356-017–8756-4

Ray, A., Hughes, L., Konisky, D. M., & Kaylor, C. (2017). Extreme weather exposure and support for climate change adaptation. *Global Environmental Change, 46*, 104–113. http://doi.org/10.1016/j.gloenvcha.2017.07.002

Reynaud, A., Aubert, C., & Nguyen, M. H. (2013). Living with floods: Protective behaviours and risk perception of Vietnamese households. *Geneva Papers on Risk and Insurance-Issues and Practice, 38*, 547–579. http://doi.org/10.1057/gpp.2013.16

Riad, J. K., Norris, F. H., & Ruback, R. B. (1999). Predicting evacuation in two major disasters: Risk perception, social influence, and access to resources. *Journal of Applied Social Psychology, 25*(5), 918–934. http://doi.org/10.1111/j.1559–1816.1999.tb00132.x

Richert, C., Erdlenbruch, K., & Figuières, C. (2017). The determinants of households' flood mitigation decisions in France – on the possibility of feedback effects from past investments. *Ecological Economics, 131*, 342–352. http://doi.org/10.1016/j.ecolecon.2016.09.014

Rincon, E., Linares, M. Y. R., & Greenberg, B. (2001). Effect of previous experience of a hurricane on preparedness for future hurricanes. *American Journal of Emergency Medicine, 19*(4), 276–279. http://doi.org/10.1053/ajem.2001.22668

Roesch-McNally, G. E., Arbuckle, J. G., & Tyndall, J. C. (2017). What would farmers do? Adaptation intentions under a Corn Belt climate change scenario. *Agriculture and Human Values, 34*, 333–346. http://doi.org/10.1007/s10460-016–9719-y

Rogers, R. W. (1975). A protection motivation theory of fear appeals and attitude change. *The Journal of Psychology, 91*, 93–114.

Rogers, R. W. (1983). Cognitive and physiological processes in fear appeals and attitude change: A revised theory of protection motivation. In B. L. Cacioppo & L. L. Petty (Eds.), *Social Psychophysiology: A Sourcebook* (pp. 153–176). London: Guildford Press.

Ruiter, R. A. C., Abraham, C., & Kok, G. (2001). Scary warnings and rational precautions: A review of the psychology of fear appeals. *Psychology & Health, 16*(6), 613–630. http://doi.org/10.1080/08870440108405863

Ruiter, R. A. C., Kessels, L. T. E., Peters, G.-J. Y., & Kok, G. (2014). Sixty years of fear appeal research: Current state of the evidence. *International Journal of Psychology, 49*(2), 63–70. http://doi.org/10.1002/ijop.12042

Sadri, A. M., Ukkusuri, S. V., & Gladwin, H. (2017). The role of social networks and information sources on hurricane evacuation decision making. *Natural Hazards Review, 18*(3), 04017005. http://doi.org/10.1061/(ASCE)NH.1527–6996.0000244

Samaddar, S., Chatterjee, R., Misra, B., & Tatano, H. (2014). Outcome-expectancy and self-efficacy: Reasons or results of flood preparedness intention? *International Journal of Disaster Risk Reduction, 8*, 91–99. http://doi.org/10.1016/j.ijdrr.2014.02.002

Sattler, D. N., Kaiser, C. F., & Hittner, J. B. (2000). Disaster preparedness: Relationships among prior experience, personal characteristics, and distress. *Journal of Applied Social Psychology, 30*(7), 1396–1420. http://doi.org/10.1111/j.1559–1816.2000.tb02527.x

Sauerborn, R., & Ebi, K. (2012). Climate change and natural disasters: Integrating science and practice to protect health. *Global Health Action, 5*, 19295. http://doi.org/10.3402/gha.v5i0.19295

Schulte, S., & Miller, K. A. (2010). Wildfire risk and climate change: The influence on homeowner mitigation behavior in the wildland–urban interface. *Society & Natural Resources, 23*, 417–435. http://doi.org/10.1080/08941920903431298

Scolobig, A., De Marchi, B., & Borga, M. (2012). The missing link between flood risk awareness and preparedness: Findings from case studies in an Alpine Region. *Natural Hazards, 63*(2), 499–520. http://doi.org/10.1007/s11069-012–0161-1

Semenza, J. C., Ploubidis, G. B., & George, L. A. (2011). Climate change and climate variability: Personal motivation for adaptation and mitigation. *Environmental Health, 10*, 46. http://doi.org/10.1186/1476-069X-10–46

Shao, W., Xian, S., Lin, N., Kunreuther, H., Jackson, N., & Goidel, K. (2017). Understanding the effects of past flood events and perceived and estimated flood risks on individuals' voluntary flood insurance purchase behavior. *Water Research, 108*, 391–400. http://doi.org/10.1016/j.watres.2016.11.021

Sharma, U., & Patt, A. (2012). Disaster warning response: The effects of different types of personal experience. *Natural Hazards, 60*, 409–423. http://doi.org/10.1007/s11069-011–0023-2

Siegrist, M., & Gutscher, H. (2008). Natural hazards and motivation for mitigation behavior: People cannot predict the affect evoked by a severe flood. *Risk Analysis, 28*(3), 771–778. http://doi.org/10.1111/j.1539–6924.2008.01049.x

Simms, J. R. Z. (2017). "Why would I live anyplace else?": Resilience, sense of place, and possibilities of migration in coastal Louisiana. *Journal of Coastal Research*, *33*(2), 408–420. http://doi.org/10.2112/JCOASTRES-D-15–00193.1

Singh, A. S., Zwickle, A., Bruskotter, J. T., & Wilson, R. (2017). The perceived psychological distance of climate change impacts and its influence on support for adaptation policy. *Environmental Science & Policy*, *73*, 93–99.

Sjöberg, L. (1998). Worry and risk perception. *Risk Analysis*, *18*(1), 85–93. http://doi.org/10.1111/j.1539–6924.1998.tb00918.x

Smit, B., Burton, I., Klein, R. J. T., & Wandel, J. (2000). An anatomy of adaptation to climate change and variability. *Climate Change*, *45*, 223–251. http://doi.org/10.1023/A:1005661622966

Soane, E., Schubert, I., Challenor, P., Lunn, R., Narendran, S., & Pollard, S. (2010). Flood perception and mitigation: The role of severity, agency, and experience in the purchase of flood protection, and the communication of flood information. *Environment and Planning A*, *42*, 3023–3038. http://doi .org/10.1068/a43238

Solomon, S., Plattner, G.-K., Knutti, R., & Friedlingstein, P. (2008). Irreversible climate change due to carbon dioxide emissions. *Proceedings of the National Academy of Sciences*, *106*(6), 1704–1709.

Steg, L. (2018). Limiting climate change requires research on climate action. *Nature Climate Change*, *8*, 759–761. http://doi.org/10.1038/s41558-018–0269-8

Steg, L., & Vlek, C. (2009). Encouraging pro-environmental behaviour: An integrative review and research agenda. *Journal of Environmental Psychology*, *29*(3), 309–317. http://doi.org/10.1016/j.jenvp.2008.10.004

Stein, R. M., Dueñas-Osorio, L., & Subramanian, D. (2010). Who evacuates when hurricanes approach? The role of risk, information, and location. *Social Science Quarterly*, *91*(3), 816–834. http://doi.org/10.1111/j.1540–6237 .2010.00721.x

Stojanov, R., Duží, B., Daněk, T., Němec, D., & Procházka, D. (2015). Adaptation to the impacts of climate extremes in central Europe: A case study in a rural area in the Czech Republic. *Sustainability*, *7*, 12758–12786. http://doi.org/10.3390/su70912758

Stoutenborough, J. W., & Vedlitz, A. (2014). The effect of perceived and assessed knowledge of climate change on public policy concerns: An empirical comparison. *Environmental Science and Policy*, *37*, 23–33. http://doi.org /10.1016/j.envsci.2013.08.002

Takao, K., Motoyoshi, T., Sato, T., Fukuzondo, T., Seo, K., & Ikeda, S. (2004). Factors determining residents' preparedness for floods in modern megalopolises: The case of the Tokai flood disaster in Japan. *Journal of Risk Research*, *7*(7–8), 775–787. http://doi.org/10.1080/1366987031000075996

Terpstra, T. (2011). Emotions, trust, and perceived risk: Affective and cognitive routes to flood preparedness behavior. *Risk Analysis*, *31*(10), 1658–1675. http://doi.org/10.1111/j.1539–6924.2011.01616.x

Terpstra, T., & Gutteling, J. M. (2008). Households' perceived responsibilities in flood risk management in the Netherlands. *International Journal of Water Resources Development*, *24*(4), 555–565. http://doi.org/10.1080/07900620801923385

Terpstra, T., & Lindell, M. K. (2012). Citizens' perceptions of flood hazard adjustments: An application of the protective action decision model. *Environment and Behavior*, *45*(8), 993–1018. http://doi.org/10.1177/0013916512452427

Thaker, J., Maibach, E., Leiserowitz, A., Zhao, X., & Howe, P. (2016). The role of collective efficacy in climate change adaptation in India. *Weather, Climate, and Society*, *8*, 21–34. http://doi.org/10.1175/WCAS-D-14–00037.1

Tibbits, A., & Whittaker, J. (2007). Stay and defend or leave early: Policy problems and experiences during the 2003 Victorian bushfires. *Environmental Hazards*, *7* (4), 283–290. http://doi.org/10.1016/j.envhaz.2007.08.001

Tierney, K. J., Lindell, M. K., & Perry, R. W. (2001). *Facing the Unexpected: Disaster Preparedness and Response in the United States*. Washington, DC: The National Academies Press. http://doi.org/10.17226/9834

Tinsley, C. H., Dillon, R. L., & Cronin, M. A. (2012). How near-miss events amplify or attenuate risky decision making. *Management Science*, *58*(9), 1596–1613. http://doi.org/10.1287/mnsc.1120.1517

Tol, R. S. J., Klein, R. J. T., & Nicholls, R. J. (2008). Towards successful adaptation to sea-level rise along Europe's coasts. *Journal of Coastal Research*, *24*(2), 432–442. http://doi.org/10.2112/07A-0016.1

Truelove, H. B., Carrico, A. R., & Thabrew, L. (2015). A socio-psychological model for analyzing climate change adaptation: A case study of Sri Lankan paddy farmers. *Global Environmental Change*, *31*, 85–97. http://doi.org/10.1016/j.gloenvcha.2014.12.010

Ung, M., Luginaah, I., Chuenpagdee, R., & Campbell, G. (2016). Perceived self-efficacy and adaptation to climate change in coastal Cambodia. *Climate*, *4*, 1. http://doi.org/10.3390/cli4010001

van Duinen, R., Filatova, T., Geurts, P., & van der Veen, A. (2015). Coping with drought risk: Empirical analysis of farmers' drought adaptation in the south-west Netherlands. *Regional Environmental Change*, *15*, 1081–1093. http://doi.org/10.1007/s10113-014–0692-y

Van Valkengoed, A. M., & Steg, L. (2019). Meta-analyses of factors motivating climate change adaptation. *Nature Climate Change*, *9*, 158–163. http://doi.org/10.1038/s41558-018–0371-y

Verplanken, B. (2006). Beyond frequency: Habit as mental construct. *British Journal of Social Psychology*, *45*, 639–656. http://doi.org/10.1348/014466605X49122

Wachinger, G., Renn, O., Begg, C., & Kuhlicke, C. (2013). The risk perception paradox - Implications for governance and communication of natural hazards. *Risk Analysis*, *33*(6), 1049–1065. http://doi.org/10.1111/j.1539–6924.2012.01942.x

Wagar, B. M., & Dixon, M. J. (2005). Past experience influences object representation in working memory. *Brain and Cognition*, *57*, 248–256. http://doi.org/10.1016/j.bandc.2004.08.054

Wamsler, C., & Brink, E. (2014). Interfacing citizens' and institutions' practice and responsibilities for climate change adaptation. *Urban Climate*, *7*, 64–91. http://doi.org/10.1016/j.uclim.2013.10.009

Weber, E. U. (2010). What shapes perceptions of climate change? *Wiley Interdisciplinary Reviews: Climate Change*, *1*, 332–342. http://doi.org/10.1002/wcc.41

Weber, E. U., & Stern, P. C. (2011). Public understanding of climate change in the United States. *American Psychologist*, *66*(4), 315–328. http://doi.org/10.1037/a0023253

Weinstein, N. D., Rothman, A. J., & Nicolich, M. (1998). Use of correlational data to examine the effects of risk perceptions on precautionary behavior. *Psychology & Health*, *13*, 479–501. http://doi.org/10.1080/08870449808407305

Wheeler, S., Zuo, A., & Bjornlund, H. (2013). Farmers' climate change beliefs and adaptation strategies for a water scarce future in Australia. *Global Environmental Change*, *23*, 537–547. http://doi.org/10.1016/j.gloenvcha.2012.11.008

Whitehead, J. C., Edwards, B., Van Willigen, M., Maiolo, J. R., Wilson, K., & Smith, K. T. (2000). Heading for higher ground: Factors affecting real and hypothetical hurricane evacuation behavior. *Environmental Hazards*, *2*, 133–142. http://doi.org/10.1016/S1464-2867(01)00013–4

Woods, B. A., Nielsen, H. Ø., Pedersen, A. B., & Kristofersson, D. (2017). Farmers' perceptions of climate change and their likely responses in Danish agriculture. *Land Use Policy*, *65*, 109–120. http://doi.org/10.1016/j.landusepol.2017.04.007

Woolfolk, J. (2018, August). As wildfire costs reach new heights, will homeowners get socked on insurance? *The Mercury News*. www.mercurynews

.com/2018/08/20/as-wildfire-costs-reach-new-heights-will-homeowners-get-socked-on-insurance/

Xian, S., Lin, N., & Hatzikyriakou, A. (2015). Storm surge damage to residential areas: A quantitative analysis for Hurricane Sandy in comparison with FEMA flood map. *Natural Hazards*, *79*, 1867–1888. http://doi.org/10.1007/s11069-015–1937-x

Yan, Y., Jacques-Tiura, A. J., Chen, X., Xie, N., Chen, J., Yang, N., . . . Kolmodin MacDonnell, K. (2014). Application of the protection motivation theory in predicting cigarette smoking among adolescents in China. *Addictive Behaviors*, *39*(1), 181–188. http://doi.org/10.1021/nn300902w.Release

Yohe, G., & Tol, R. S. J. (2002). Indicators for social and economic coping capacity – Moving toward a working definition of adaptive capacity. *Global Environmental Change*, *12*(1), 25–40. www.sciencedirect.com/science/article/B6VFV-44PKMW2-1/2/3ee8b23c9aa2f471209673d68e60e1c6

Yung, L., Phear, N., DuPont, A., Montag, J., & Murphy, D. (2015). Drought adaptation and climate change beliefs among working ranchers in Montana. *Weather, Climate, and Society*, *7*, 281–293. http://doi.org/10.1175/WCAS-D-14–00039.1

Zaalberg, R., Midden, C., Meijnders, A., & McCalley, T. (2009). Prevention, adaptation, and threat denial: Flooding experiences in the Netherlands. *Risk Analysis*, *29*(12), 1759–1778. http://doi.org/10.1111/j.1539–6924.2009.01316.x

Zhang, W., Wang, W., Lin, J., Zhang, Y., Shang, X., Wang, X., . . . Ma, W. (2017). Perception, knowledge and behaviors related to typhoon: A cross sectional study among rural residents in Zhejiang, China. *International Journal of Environmental Research and Public Health*, *14*, 492. http://doi.org/10.3390/ijerph14050492

## Cambridge Elements

# Applied Social Psychology

Susan Clayton
*College of Wooster, Ohio*

Susan Clayton is a social psychologist at the College of Wooster in Wooster, Ohio. Her research focuses on the human relationship with nature, how it is socially constructed, and how it can be utilized to promote environmental concern.



**About the Series**

Many social psychologists have used their research to understand and address pressing social issues, from poverty and prejudice to work and health. Each Element in this series reviews a particular area of applied social psychology. Elements will also discuss applications of the research findings and describe directions for future study.

Cambridge Elements

# Applied Social Psychology

## Elements in the Series

*Empathy and Concern with Negative Evaluation in Intergroup Relations: Implications for Designing Effective Interventions*
Jacquie D. Vorauer

*The Psychology of Climate Change Adaptation*
Anne van Valkengoed and Linda Steg

A full series listing is available at: www.cambridge.org/EASP

CPSIA information can be obtained
at www.ICGtesting.com
Printed in the USA
LVHW030816130120
643322LV00014B/385/P

9 781108 724456